VANCOUVER ISLAND

Book of **Musts**

The 101 Places Every Islander MUST See

D0700804

If you think you know Vancouver Island, think again

Peter Grant

TO OUR READERS

Every effort has been made by authors and editors to ensure that the information enclosed in this book is accurate and up-to-date. We revise and update annually, however, many things can change after a book gets published. If you discover any out-of-date or incorrect information in the Vancouver Island Book of Musts, we would appreciate hearing from you via our website at www.bookofeverything.com.

Copyright 2016 by MacIntyre Purcell Publishing Inc.

MacIntyre Purcell Publishing Inc.
232 Lincoln St., PO Box 1142
Lunenburg, Nova Scotia
B0J 2C0 Canada
www.bookofeverything.com
info@bookofeverything.com

We acknowledge the support of the Department of Canadian Heritage and the Nova Scotia Department of Tourism, Culture and Heritage in the development of writing and publishing in Canada.

Cover photo: Runner on Victoria waterfront with Olympic Mountains behind - Boomer Jerritt/All Canada Photos
Author photo by Godfrey Stephens.

Printed and bound in Canada
Library and Archives Canada Cataloguing in Publication

Grant, Peter, 1948-
Vancouver Island book of musts : the 101 places every islander must see / Peter Grant.

Issued also in electronic format.
ISBN 978-0-9810941-6-8

1. Vancouver Island (B.C.)--Guidebooks. I. Title.

FC3844.2.G74 2010   917.11'2045   C2010-905030-4

MIX
Paper from
responsible sources
FSC® C103567

Introduction

Welcome to the Vancouver Island 101 — our best places.

My list is a composite. It's got many of the islands' superlative and unique places, for sure. It includes some of our icons, a few places that are just plain favorites, and a few that snuck in by a mysterious process. Call it buzz. Goats on the roof. In some places a window opens on history, while another locates a story of our tribe. The list is organized geographically, as if you were on a tour. It avoids any suggestion of priority. That would be mixing apples and oranges.

Vancouver Island is a diverse land, and almost as much sea as land, with true rainforests on the exposed west side, and places on the more protected east side where cactuses grow. The big island is 454 kilometres from end to end and an average 80 km wide, with a rugged mountain spine down the middle. Factor in the Gulf and Discovery islands, Broughton Archipelago and the islands to north and west, and this remarkable section of Canada's west coast measures up at 33,650 square kilometres.

Inhabited by First Nations for thousands of years, Vancouver Island was discovered by Europeans in the 18th century and, in the 19th, colonized, settled, governed and exploited by the British empire and its successors the governments of British Columbia and Canada. Our population totals 748,984, according to the 2009 estimate. Ninety percent of us live in the southeast quarter.

Vancouver Island is best known for wild nature, wilderness, big trees, old-growth forests, wildlife and wild fish. Some of these Musts are included with the advice to see them while you can. A few are places neither you nor I will ever see — they're too remote, or access is restricted — but they're deemed important just to know about. One Must isn't a place at all. Wild salmon represent the totality of Vancouver Island as no single place or other thing.

Vancouver Island is famous for its wilderness experiences. Some of the best places involve challenging self-propelled travel. On a general note, anyone undertaking such excursions should be well-prepared and well-equipped, with a guide if necessary. We treasure our islands' many beauties, love to share them, and hope that their visitors will be inspired to practice low-impact travel. If you bring it in, please take it out!

We are fortunate to share these islands with peoples who have a radically different take on nature, history, culture and society. This book celebrates the richness of First Nations culture, one of the great achievements of these islands.

Blessed by nature, the islands are full of people who know what to do with soil and sunlight and how to set a table. Our many notable establishments could easily have their own Book of Musts.

Sincere thanks are due to the many people who provided information and helped fill in the details about these extraordinary places, especially the contributors of Take Fives.

Special thanks to publisher John Macintyre — whose crazy, wonderful idea this book is — for the freedom to write about matters dear to my heart.

And to Paula, companion of many travels and the larger journey, for the support and encouragement that made it possible.

TABLE OF CONTENTS

GONZALES HILL (PETER GRANT)

6

Victoria and Southern Vancouver Island

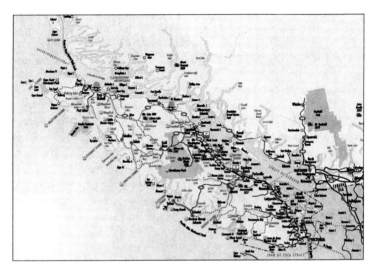

Southern Vancouver Island includes Victoria, Sooke (35 kilometres southwest) and the Saanich Peninsula (35 km north). The Strait of Juan de Fuca is at its feet, and the Sooke Hills and Highlands form the backdrop. It's an area with a remarkable spectrum of climatic conditions — from Sooke's *wet coast* feel to Sidney's rain-shadow heat trap. The traditional home of Salish First Nations, Victoria was where the English colonial project started in 1843. It grew from a little trading depot to include three cities, two towns and eight municipal districts. Victoria has been a seat of government since 1849 and the capital of British Columbia since 1868. Esquimalt has had a naval base since the 1850s. A host of outstanding cultural and heritage sites are based on these twin heritages. The economic wealth reflected in the area's fine homes, gardens and restaurants is matched by the riches of its parks and natural areas — within hailing distance of the 375,000 people who call it home.

Songhees Point 1

The austere simplicity of ancient rock gives Songhees Point, on the west side of Victoria's Inner Harbour, an elemental character. It is a fitting place to contemplate the history of Victoria's First Nations.

A bronze sculpture represents a spindle whorl, an icon of the Coast Salish people and an important piece of traditional Salish wool-spinning technology.

The casting is the work of local First Nations artist Butch Dick. It's one of seven Signs of Lekwungen installed around Victoria to mark sites of significance to First Peoples. Each has a different motif. This one's is salmon — an essential part of First Peoples' traditional diet. This waterway once had runs of salmon.

The First Nations account of Victoria's history is not well known. I'm trying to get the names and stories straight.

A display near the point profiles the Lekwungen First Nation.

Songhees was the Europeans' name for the First Nations who gathered around Fort Victoria and settled on the west side of the harbour. Songhees Village stood about where the Ocean Pointe Hotel now stands. At first there were many more indigenous people than European.

The traditional name of the local indigenous people was *Lekwungen*. Their old villages were located in protected areas along 50 km of coast between Metchosin and Saanich and on the waterway above the harbour. Six or seven families owned the land and its resources. Their territorial boundaries were described in the Fort Victoria treaties of 1850-52.

The Lekwungen and other local First Nations sold their lands forever to the Queen of England for a total of £107, retaining the right to use their traditional territories for hunting and fishing.

The village coexisted with the city for more than 60 years. Gradually, the area around Songhees Village, although designated an Indian Reserve, filled in with industries and institutional buildings.

A solution to the encroachment was reached in 1912 whereby the nation sold their land again and resettled on Esquimalt Harbour.

Hard to believe — the shores of Victoria Harbour were once filled with smokestacks. Songhees Point was dominated by Sidney Rubber Roofing's asphalt shingle plant. Up the hill was an oil tank farm.

Songhees Point is now part of the Westsong Walkway linear park — a 2.7 km walk from the Johnson St bridge to West Bay.

There are good views of the façades of old Victoria — some buildings go back to the 1850s — the tourist hub around the Empress Hotel, and the legislative precinct further along. To the south is the suburb of James Bay and to the west, across the outer harbour, the Esquimalt shore.

Details: *Signs of Lekwungen: http://www.victoria.ca/cityhall/comdev_ccc_wlkwy.shtml. Self-guided tour.*
Reading: Songhees Pictorial: A History of the Songhees People as seen by Outsiders 1790-1912 *by Grant Keddie (Royal British Columbia Museum, 2003). Keddie is the museum's curator of archaeology.*

2   The Steps of the BC Parliament Buildings

From East to West the circling word has passed,
Till West is East beside our land-locked blue;
From East to West the tested chain holds fast,
The well-forged link rings true!

That strange little ditty is called *Victoria*. It's from the 1896 poem The Song of the Cities by Rudyard Kipling.

Kipling's jingo-lingo was the versical equivalent of the British Columbia Parliament Buildings. Both were conceived as propaganda for the British Empire. When the Ledge was completed in 1898, BC had fewer than 100,000 souls.

The Hudson's Bay Company established a toe-hold here in 1843. By 1849 Fort Victoria was capital of the colony of Vancouver Island. By 1862 it was a city, by 1868 the capital of British Columbia, which in 1871 became the sixth province in the Canadian Confederation.

From a grassy field to the metropolis of a vast hinterland measuring 950,000 sq km — larger than France and Italy combined — within 30 years. (Today BC's population approaches 4.5 million, while France and Italy together have 122 million.)

The centre of power in the province is the Premier's Office. The Premier is the province's chief executive officer, and has almost untrammeled authority to run BC's affairs. In the parliamentary system, the executive branch controls the legislature, the law-making body.

Here's how former BC premier Bill Vander Zalm (1986-91) put it in the Victoria *Times-Colonist* in 2010: "I don't recall ever seeing democracy in this province, or any other province or the country. We always elect a dictator and for four years a dictator determined what was. I'll qualify that a little bit by saying, fortunately, for the most part we've elected benevolent dictators."

Our democratic rights may have become clouded by electoral dictatorship, but the right of peaceful protest endures, based on hallowed principles of free assembly and free speech.

The steps of the Ledge are where protesters gather to demonstrate — ordinary citizens joining voices against the executive steamroller. From gatherings of unemployed workers during the Great Depression to the pro- and anti-logging demonstrations of the 1990s. First Nations groups, advocates for children with autism, health care workers concerned about budgetary cutbacks. They come from all over to protest against unregulated fish farms, privatized tree farms, private deals for power projects.

The steps of the Ledge are one place where democracy is alive.

CPR Steamship Terminal   3

Ferries are a fact of life for islanders. The government-operated BC Ferry fleet is our marine highway system. The latest models are decked out like cruise ships. But turn back the clock, and the Inner Harbour fills up with tiny ocean liners wreathed in black smoke. A liquid steam whistle announces a departure.

For more than 50 years the Canadian Pacific Railway (CPR) maintained a fleet of handsome coastal steamers known as the Princess ships. Their Victoria docks were beside the pillared CPR Steamship Terminal on Belleville St. It was Victoria's temple of transport.

Princess Ship Roll Call! — *Victoria! Beatrice! Charlotte! Adelaide! Mary! Alice! Patricia! Marguerite! Sophia! Maquinna! Irene! Margaret! Louise! Kathleen! Elaine! Norah! Elizabeth! Joan! Marguerite II! Patricia II!* (There were others; they don't fit this mold.)

The larger ships, weighing 5,000-6,000 tons gross, offered comfortable, fast, frequent sailings to Vancouver and Seattle and, in the 1920s, summer cruises to Alaska.

The Princesses *Maquinna* and *Norah* provided essential services to isolated Vancouver Island communities.

Over time the ships' designs morphed into the modern, and the names lost that quaint quality. The last ones built were the *Princess of Nanaimo* (1951) and *Princess of Vancouver* (1955).

An early memory: being hoisted into the arms of an old man beside a stone wall. That was my grandfather. It's my only memory of my grandparents. Grandfather was standing by the Inner Harbour causeway, I guess, about to catch the Night Boat to Vancouver. He made the long train trip from Owen Sound, Ontario to meet my sister and brother and I. We were his only grandchildren — my father's four siblings all died before my time.

I took the Night Boat once with my family. You went aboard the *Princess Joan* in the evening and settled into your room. While you slept the boat slipped its moorings. In the morning you went on deck to find the boat already gliding under the Lion's Gate Bridge into Vancouver Harbour.

I sailed to Seattle on the *Princess Patricia II* to attend the World's Fair, an afternoon sailing that allowed me and my friend to stay aboard overnight. We had to clear out of our room early but could return in the evening. For 14-year-old boys, it doesn't get any better.

I sailed on the *Princess Marguerite II* when she was 40 years old and in a sorry state. Sheer nostalgia kept her on the Seattle-Victoria tourist run until 1989. The *Princess of Vancouver* survived until 1991.

We loved the Princess ships. We'll never see their likes again.

The Steamship Terminal's commercial tenant vacated in 2010, making possible its restoration as a transportation hub.

Reading: *Robert D. Turner's* The Pacific Princesses: An Illustrated History of the Canadian Pacific Railway's Princess Fleet on the Northwest Coast *(Victoria: Sono Nis Press, 1977, many reprints).*

4 | Tea Lobby, Fairmont Empress Hotel

The elegant Tea Lobby of the Fairmont Empress Hotel is famous for Afternoon Tea.

In olden days the Tea Lobby was known as the Lounge — and thereby hangs this tale of a fateful encounter.

It begins on the Saturday evening after Christmas, when the Empress is decked out in festive greens. There's a big dinner party in the Crystal Ballroom. Victoria's businessmen are singing "For He's a Jolly Good Fellow."

In the Lounge, a hotel guest is visiting with a local friend. She will describe "the sounds of revelry and singing" in a letter that surfaces 12 years later in the *London Daily Express.*

They peek into the Ballroom. The friend discovers that "the honoured guest, the man who had inspired this outburst, was an acquaintance." The banquet breaks up. Some of the diners move to the Lounge. "K. introduced me to his acquaintance," the visitor would write.

The acquaintance is Francis Rattenbury — merely the architect of the BC Parliament Buildings while in his 20s and creator of the Empress Hotel in his 30s.

The noted Canadian architect, now 55 year old, is introduced to a young woman named Alma Clarke. She is a classical concert pianist with a knack for writing and selling popular songs. She grew up in Kamloops but is a woman of the World. Widowed in World War I, she drove ambulances on the battlefield in Salonika, Greece. She was decorated for bravery. Now she is a single mother.

"You have almost the kindest face I ever saw," she says when they happen to meet at a party.

Rattenbury's 25-year marriage is unhappy. Husband and wife live apart in their Oak Bay waterfront paradise, communicating mostly through their daughter.

Alma and Ratz (as he was known to friends) conduct an affair with little regard for the scandal that erupts. A divorce ensues. Ratz and Alma marry and have a child. Victoria society shuns them, and Rattenbury cannot get work. His debts pile up.

They flee with their two children, settling in Bournemouth, on England's southwest coast. Besides the children, Alma has a live-in companion and, beginning in September 1934, a 17-year-old "chauffeur/handyman" named Robert Stoner.

Rattenbury, now in his late 60s, drinks heavily and is depressed. He often threatens suicide. "Well, get on with it," Alma teases. She loves him dearly, the companion will testify. The thing is, there's no romance — they have an Arrangement.

In November, having turned 18, Stoner moves in. He is seduced by Alma, and they become lovers. They run away to London, where Alma lavishes gifts on him in what the Court will call *an orgy*. A doctor will testify that she has flare-ups of tuberculosis, which can induce *nymphomania*.

Two days after their return from London, Alma makes plans to take the ailing Francis to see a doctor in a nearby town.

Stoner becomes inflamed with jealousy. That very evening he borrows a mallet from his grandfather and bludgeons Francis in his easy chair.

Driven mad with grief and yet desperate to protect her lover, Alma confesses to the crime. Alma and Stoner are tried together for murder. The four-day trial electrifies the country. Stoner is found guilty and sentenced to hang. Alma is acquitted but soon takes her own life, having lost her husband, lover and reputation.

The British public is moved to pity for the young Stoner. Alma Rattenbury is seen as having used sex to dominate a mere boy. Even the slain architect is an object of contempt for winking at his wife's affairs. Stoner's sentence is commuted and he is out of prison within seven years.

A modern tragedy. It all started here. Enjoy your tea!

Details: *Visitors are welcome to stroll around the heritage lobby of the Fairmont Empress Hotel; enter by the porte cochère near Government and Belleville. Reservations (250-389-2727) are a must for Afternoon Tea; expect to pay well over $50CDN; dress code; to be seated in the Tea Lobby in high season, book well in advance.*
Readings: *Terry Reksten,* Rattenbury *(1978) and* The Fairmont Empress: The First Hundred Years *(revised ed. 2008).*

Royal BC Museum and Thunderbird Park   5

I've been visiting the Royal BC Museum for half a century. In the exhibits hall I cut to the chase: third floor, First Peoples.

The First Peoples exhibit is endlessly fascinating — simply the most accessible way I know to begin understanding BC's indigenous heritage. The sequence on the effects of European contact is guaranteed to make you think.

The displays were created in the 1970s with the collaboration of dozens of First Nations people. Detailed woodwork down to the handrails was honed by the artistic Hunt family of the Fort Rupert Kwakiutl First Nation. There is a scaled-down walk-in model of a big-house built by Henry Hunt and his sons Tony and Richard.

The museum complex has other notable parts. The tower houses workers who collect, study and curate — little-seen foundations of the Museum. Its mission since 1886 is "to preserve specimens of the natural products and Indian antiquities and manufactures of the Province and to classify and exhibit the same for the information of the public."

Among the Museum's men and women of science are some legendary field workers — Charles Newcombe, Frank Kermode, Wilson Duff.

The BC Archives, by the sunken courtyard, is an indispensable resource for historians and genealogists. The reference room is one of the most useful in the city.

On the Belleville St. side of the exhibit building are glassed displays of original carved monumental art from coastal villages. Of the weathered masterworks, a human-sized Cowichan house figure of the 19th century stands out for its iconic simplicity.

To me the most fascinating part of the whole complex is the painted house in Thunderbird Park. It's the centerpiece of a huge presence of Kwakiutl artists in Victoria that continues to this day. The builder of the house was paterfamilias and principal exponent.

Mungo Martin (c1881-1962) trained in carving and painting, dancing, singing and storytelling in his native Fort Rupert, where Kwakwaka'wakw traditions survived intact. He collected a museum's-worth of artifacts and folkways. Mungo had several chiefly titles, some inherited and some acquired. One was *Nakapankam*, Ten Times a Chief.

After a life in commercial fishing, Mungo Martin took a post at the University of British Columbia to carve poles and teach the arts. He moved to Victoria in 1952 to be carver-in-residence at the Museum and settled here.

Martin and Henry Hunt, his son-in-law, replicated many of the poles in Thunderbird Park. It was a repository of original monumental art, but the old poles were deteriorating. Their replicas comprise much of the collection in the park today.

Mungo Martin House, built in 1953, is a scaled-down version of a Fort Rupert big house. Its four interior houseposts are elaborately carved with the owner's heraldic crests. The RBCM website has a good historical account of the big house and the park.

A bit further afield in Beacon Hill Park is the 39-metre pole Mungo Martin put up in 1956. The *world's tallest totem pole* is so well loved it was taken down in 2000, restored, recarved, repainted and remounted.

Think of it — a modest fisherman in bluejean overalls, a local yokel, was really this cultural dynamo whose stature as an artist is difficult to overstate. Among those who Mungo Martin influenced were Bill Reid and Doug Cranmer. His protégé Tony Hunt and Tony's brother Richard Hunt are artists of standing who make their homes in Victoria. The next generation is already well-established and their work known worldwide.

When I reflect on the contribution of the Kwakiutl First Nation, with their living connection to ancient north island cultures, it seems to me one of our strongest legacies.

Did I say *our*? Whether it's ours or theirs, it's alive and kicking in Victoria.

Details: *Royal British Columbia Museum, 675 Belleville St, Victoria; (250) 356-7226 or toll free 1-888-447-7977; royalbcmuseum.bc.ca. Other exhibits: natural history, modern* *history; IMAX Theatre, café, a splendid bookstore; Helmcken House (built 1852) nearby. BC Archives, 655 Beleville St: bcarchives.bc.ca. The online visual records database is an outstanding historical research tool. Register in person to use the reference room.*

6   Blue Bridge

An antique blue bridge spans Victoria Harbour and makes a western portal to the Old Town. Locals love the old contraption.

The Johnson St. Bridge is really two — it has separate vehicle and railway spans. There's a stream of bike and pedestrian users.

When a vessel of a certain height approaches, all traffic grinds to a halt, a siren wails, lights flash, barriers descend, decks rise, counterweights fall.

Up and down — that must be why it's called a *bascule bridge*. Bascule is French for "seesaw."

Built in 1924, the Blue Bridge requires a foundational overhaul. The City proposed replacing it, but that provoked an unprecedented public outpouring. Unfortunately, it would cost more to keep than to replace the Blue Bridge, and a budget for a fixed span will soon be put to the citizens.

The bridge is a part of the historic Lower Johnson (LoJo) streetscape and Market Square façade, where you can see the ghostly lettering of a sign painted on the front of a grain warehouse.

The tiny VIA rail station is the terminus of the Esquimalt and Nanaimo Railway. It may soon be on the other side of the harbour — no room on the new bridge.

Across the tracks is the empty Janion building, offices of the E&N Railway until 1948. The City is trying to protect the building while the property is on the market. The hope is to find a buyer who will invest in its rehabilitation as part of a commercial development.

Enjoy the Blue Bridge and its surroundings while you can. Change is in the air.

Details: *The City's Johnson St Bridge site: http://www.johnsonstreetbridge.com/.*

Chinatown   7

Victoria's Chinatown is centred on the lower block of Fisgard St. and covers about eight blocks. Fisgard St. has a terrific atmosphere — neon-lit restaurants, grocery shops with produce spilling over the sidewalks and an old-fashioned Chinese butcher, side by side with art galleries and funky clothiers. It's one of the most vibrant parts of Old Town.

Chinatown flourished during and after construction of the Canadian

Pacific Railway. It's the oldest and was once the largest Chinatown in Canada. The whole area was honeycombed with secret passageways. Fan Tan Alley, the wonderfully narrow passage between Fisgard and Pandora Ave, is suggestive of that architecture. A diversity of little retail shops lines the shadowy way. My favorite is The Turntable, a music store with vintage LPs.

Chinatown went into a long decline before its fortunes revived in the 1970s. Thanks to some local initiatives the inner-city area has become liveable again.

A distinctive element of Chinatown design is the door on the street that leads to multiple apartments with open-air commons. One such complex is Dragon Alley, 532 Fisgard, across from Bean Around the World. It has been renovated into an interesting mix of residential, commercial and retail uses. The passage leads to Herald St, the beginning of another funky retail shopping zone.

Working as an election enumerator one year, I met aging residents of Chinatown who, although born in Victoria, needed an interpreter.

Chinatown, a monument to tenacity, reminds me of the different stories some Canadians tell.

Details: *Forbidden City self-guided walking tour: http://www.victoria.ca/visitors/ pdfs/wlkngt_frbddn3.pdf*
Discover the Past walking tours: http://www.discoverthepast.com/
Victoria's Chinatown, a BC Archives photo essay: http://www.bcarchives.gov. bc.ca/sn-32805B/exhibits/timemach/galler02/frames/chinatown2.htm
Reading: The Secret City within Victoria *by David Chuenyan Lai. Out of print.*
Bean Around the World, 533 Fisgard St, Victoria; buys Central American coffees from producers: http://www.cowboycoffee.ca/batworganicroasts.html

8 John's Place Restaurant

John's Place is the Victoria restaurant most likely to have a line-up out the door late in the morning. It's famous for breakfast, particularly Eggs Benedict, which owner John Cantin says outsells the rest of the menu 8 to 1. The hollandaise is from scratch, and they make their own mayonnaise, too. The runner-up in popularity is the Bottomless Bowl of Soup.

John's Place has an ambience I would call hippie. Piney-wood walls are festooned with photographs and posters like exclamation marks. It is the kind of place where the server, who's been there for 20 years, calls you honey.

John is quick to point out he is too young to have been a hippie — even though, when he motored north from LA in the early 80s to seek his fortune, it was in a 60s VW van, the rare roll-up *rag top* model. John is a collector. He treasures the artifacts of that time.

Years ago a college buddy and his wife came to visit from Ontario. We are of hippie vintage, so naturally we went to John's Place. At that time there was a functioning Wurlitzer jukebox with consoles in the booths. Marjorie, an antiques dealer, went into ecstasies.

At John's Place I like to touch spirits with two previous tenants, both pioneering Canadian photographers. Richard Maynard (1832-1907) travelled around BC as a bootmaker — think of all those miners, loggers, ranchers — and found time to photograph the evolving landscapes of the young province. The restaurant was his boot shop beginning in 1892.

Hannah Hatherly Maynard (1834-1918) was a studio photographer — her studio was upstairs — and a pioneering photographic artist who experimented with surreal techniques long before Surrealism. Her outdoor work captured the social and cultural life of the city.

Between them, the Maynards open windows on BC's past. A few of their pictures are on the walls at John's Place.

Details: *John's Place, 723 Pandora Avenue, Victoria. Open 7 am-9 pm, an hour later on week-ends, and does take reservations for 4 or more. The history of the restaurant is recounted on the hippe-style website www.johnsplace.ca.*
BC Archives' holdings of the Maynards' huge body of work can be viewed at www. bcarchives.bc.ca, under Search Visual Records.

Emily of Beacon Hill   9

Beacon Hill is the southerly prominence in Beacon Hill Park, Victoria's 82-hectare civic pleasure grounds. It has splendid views across the Strait of Juan de Fuca. There are remnants of First Nations burial tumuli on the south slope. In the early days of European settlement, beacons were lit on the hill to warn ships away from the shallows of Brochie Ledge.

Beacon Hill's greater significance is as the home range of the artist and writer Emily Carr (1871-1945). Carr's home was half a kilometre west of here. She lived 18 years on a 4-ha property between James Bay and the Dallas Road cliffs. She recounted her charmed early life in an exquisite memoir, *The Book of Small.*

Carr was tied to her home turf by temperament and fortune. She would leave only to return.

She painted from an early age. At length she grew discouraged and all but gave up art. She built an apartment house on a lot carved out of the family property and, at age 41, settled in there for 23 years.

When she was 56 and had been a rooming-house operator for 15 years, a door opened. She found a new style and a new theme. She painted forests. She painted clearcuts, too — for the sky, the light, the energy, the power.

At length she moved a few blocks away and, three years later, relocated to the house her sister Alice built where the family's vegetable garden used to be. Her last abode was St Mary's Priory — now the James Bay Inn

— a block from the family home.

We can glimpse this *small world* in the journals she kept from 1927 to 1941, edited and published posthumously as *Hundreds and Thousands*.

Carr often visited Beacon Hill Park to sketch and paint the cliffs, the sea, the Olympic Mountains and the sky. I can see her striding up the tunnels in the brush on the back slope of Beacon Hill — with Koko, Maybbe and Tantrum bounding ahead — to study the light on the strait and, if it's good, make a sketch or a watercolour.

Advice to artists from the journal for November 3, 1932:

Search for the reality of each object, that is, its real and only beauty; recognize our relationship with all life; say to every animate and inanimate thing 'brother;' be at one with all things, finding the divine in all; when one can do all this, maybe then one can paint. In the meantime one must go steadily on with open mind, courageously alert, waiting always for a lead, constantly watching, constantly praying, meditating much and not worrying.

... not worrying about, for instance, success? She must have cared. The next lines of the entry are from the poem Song of the Rolling Earth by Walt Whitman. It's an exhortation to artists to "pile up the words of the earth!/Work on, age after age, nothing is to be lost." Out rolls this Blakean prophesy: "When the materials are all prepared and ready, the architects shall appear."

Whitman's poem composes the triumph of art:

I swear to you the architects shall appear without fail,
I swear to you they will understand you and justify you,
The greatest thing among them shall be he who best knows you, and encloses all and is faithful to all,
He and the rest shall not forget you, they shall perceive that you are not an iota less than they.
You shall be fully glorified in them.

It came, a little, in her lifetime — first for her writing. After her time it was more her painting. And the circle widened.

Details: *Carr House, 207 Government St, Emily Carr's birthplace, built about 1862; open seasonally; guided tours, occasional events; see www.emilycarr.com.*
Art Gallery of Greater Victoria, 1040 Moss St, has a standing exhibit of Carr's work and life; see aggv.bc.ca.
Carr's written works are published by Douglas & McIntyre (www.dmpibooks.com). Three classics published in Carr's time: Klee Wyck *(1941),* The Book of Small *(1942) and* The House of All Sorts *(1944).*
About Beacon Hill Park, see www.victoria.ca/cityhall/departments_compar_prkbcn.shtml.

TAKE 5 BEST VICTORIA
RESTAURANTS

According to *Vancouver* magazine's Urban Diner 2009 awards and *EAT* magazine's 1st Annual Exceptional Eats! Awards. *Vancouver's* judges agreed with *EAT's* readers' poll on the first four. Excerpted suggestions are *Vancouver's.*

1. Brasserie L'Ecole
1715 Government St (250) 475-6260
". . . French country cooking with local ingredients and ace service . . . reservations mandatory . . . Beer-braised duck legs in a delicate broth of chickpeas and summer vegetables [with] truffled basil purée . . . cured pork loin [with] sauté of transparent apples, bacon, kale, and fingerling potatoes . . ."

2. Cafe Brio
944 Fort St (250) 383-0009
". . . menu changes weekly (even daily) to reflect what's fresh and available . . . sweetbread-stuffed ravioli with grilled scallions in a red-wine sauce . . . local lamb stuffed with lamb kidneys, pine nuts, and ricotta cheese over a ragout of favas, morels, and fingerling potatoes . . ."

3. Zambri's
110 – 911 Yates St (250) 360-1171
". . . vitello tonnato is seductively rich . . . local rockfish with pepperonata . . . beef striploin with gorgonzola fonduta and truffle oil . . . cauliflower allasabbia."

4. Stage
1307 Gladstone Ave (250) 388-4222
". . . langos, a savoury Hungarian fry bread . . . with Maldon sea salt and garlic or slathered with artichokes, tomatoes, and goat cheese . . ."

5. Marina Restaurant
1327 Beach Dr (250) 598-8555
". . . porcini-crusted halibut with chorizo sausage, sweet potato hash, sweet garlic purée, and braised greens . . ."

10 Craigdarroch Castle

Craigdarroch Castle is a Victoria landmark, a sandstone apparition of turrets and red tile roofs rising out of the oaks as you look up the Fort St hill.

Completed in 1888 for the Robert Dunsmuir family, it was the city's finest home, surrounded by 11 hectares of gardens and woods.

Much reduced and after many changes of hands, it pays its way as a heritage museum with sumptuous architectural details and interesting displays of Dunsmuir family history.

The Castle's exhibits pay respect to its many uses. It was a convalescent hospital during World War I. During the Great Depression it was Victoria College — Pierre Berton a notable alumnus. It was a school district office.

During the 1960s the Castle was the home of the Victoria School (now Conservatory) of Music. There were concerts in the spacious front parlour. I fell in love with string quartets there.

At the helm was a team of gifted teachers, Robin Wood and Winnifred Scott Wood. The Woods — he from Esquimalt, she from Winnipeg — met en route to England. Both were bound for the Royal College of Music to study piano.

They were talented musicians, and they fell in love. They launched a brilliant concert career together, playing duets in the capitals of Europe. Then they gave it all up to take charge of the newly-formed school of music.

The Woods devoted 35 years to building a pillar of community education with some 1800 students and alumni the likes of Jon Kimura Parker and Richard Margison.

Long story short, the Castle has an outstanding record of public service — ironic, considering it was built as a tycoon's advertisement of wealth.

Details: *Craigdarroch Castle, 1050 Joan Crescent, Victoria; (250) 592-5323; http://www.craigdarrochcastle.com.*
Victoria Conservatory of Music, 900 Johnson St, Victoria; (250) 386-5311; http://www.vcm.bc.ca/. Alix Goolden Performance Hall, 907 Pandora Ave, has probably the best acoustics in the city.

Government House Grounds 11

Government House is a 100-room mansion surrounded by 14.6 hectares of gardens and woodlands. The residence of the Queen's representative in British Columbia is not open to casual visitors, but the grounds are.

What a piece of nature this is, a magnificent public resource just a 20-minute walk east of downtown Victoria.

The spacious front and sides comprise 5.7 hectares of duck ponds, rockeries, rose gardens, herb gardens, cut flower gardens, amazing borders of perennials shaded by graceful walnut and tulip trees along the front wall. The lawns, so popular for wedding photo shoots, are edged by Douglas firs. There is a field with a bandshell, a nursery, pathways and benches and much more besides.

The grounds are conducive to contemplation. One of my favorite spots is the Sunken Garden on the west side, overlooking serpentine Lotbinière Ave with its rockery walls and a lovely Garry oak meadow below.

The south side of Government House is near the edge of a low rock escarpment. It's got one of the best views in town, overlooking the seaside suburb of Fairfield and the Strait of Juan de Fuca. There are some charming grassy spots, and to sit on a rocky knoll amid the dwarf Garry oaks is very Vancouver Island.

Below the escarpment is nearly 9 hectares of Garry oak woodland with pathways and interpretive signs.

Most inspiring to me is the small army of volunteer gardeners in the Friends of the Government House Grounds. The society was formed in the 1990s to restore the gardens after a period of government belt-tightening and neglect. They are flourishing under its care.

Details: *Government House, 1401 Rockland Ave, Victoria; http://www.ltgov.bc.ca/. Grounds open during daylight hours. Tours.*

12   Ross Bay Cemetery

"It is a rotten world, artful politicians are its bane. It's saving grace is the artlessness of the young and the wonders of the sky."

John Dean's epitaph makes a powerful statement — even with a comma splice, a misspelled word and faulty grammar. When it was finished and the gravestone set in place at the Ross Bay Cemetery, Dean posed beside it. At 86 he still had a few years left to practice his eccentricities.

Ross Bay Cemetery, established 1872 in an 11-hectare setting in Fairfield, is the shaded park-like resting place of James Douglas, Emily Carr and a who's who of Victorians early and late.

John Dean (1850-1943) was a sometime politician himself — he was mayor of Rossland, BC (1903-4). A carpenter by trade, he was always a failed politician in Victoria, where he lived his last 35 years. The native of England was a confirmed bachelor and an inveterate traveler.

Dean is best known for a park on the slopes of Mt Newton in North Saanich. He bought 32 hectares of mostly old growth forest there and built a handsome cabin where he stayed in the summer. He donated the land to the Province in 1921. Some neighbours followed suit, and John Dean Provincial Park now protects 173 hectares of forest. The Depression-era stairs and other stonework is enchanting.

The cemetery, besides being one of the most interesting and well-loved landscapes in the city, is close to the haunts of the oudoorsy.

South across Dallas Rd is Ross Bay, with views across the Strait of Juan de Fuca to the Olympic Mountains. An exquisite pebble beach is hidden beyond the steps at the east end.

To the west is a long causeway and Clover Point. A bit inland and west of the cemetery is Moss Rock, a gem of an outcrop with vistas of Victoria's south coast.

Details: *Ross Bay Cemetery, 1495 Fairfield Rd, Victoria (across from Fairfield Plaza, a shopping centre with every convenience.) Consult the Old Cemeteries Society of Victoria (www.oldcem.bc.ca) for historical information, a map and self-guiding tour of Ross Bay Cemetery and a schedule of its guided tours of Victoria's cemeteries. Information about John Dean Provincial Park, maps, directions: http://www.env.gov.bc.ca/bcparks/explore/parkpgs/john_dean/.*

Gonzales Hill   13

Gonzales Hill is a rocky eminence that rises to 66 metres above sea level on Victoria's south coast. One end looms over Gonzales Bay and the other over McNeill Bay. Little lanes run up the back and along the ridge. Houses are perched on the edges of cliffs.

The white meteorological observatory is a prominent landmark high on the rocks. Built in 1914, it was the city's weather station for decades. Today a 1.8-hectare park surrounds it. Between clumps of shore pines are picture-postcard views of Gonzales Bay.

At the east end of the ridge is rugged 2-hectare Walbran Park, with little Garry oaks, arbutus and Douglas fir. At the foot of the steps to a cairn is a large plaque with an detailed historical sketch — in bronze — of the exploration of Juan de Fuca Strait. The cairn commemorates Captain John Walbran, a resident of Gonzales Hill and author of *British Columbia Coast Names*. (It's still in print after 104 years.)

Across the road is a lookout dating from World War II, with magnificent views in every direction. It overlooks King George Terrace Harling Point and, just offshore, the Trial Islands.

This landscape — a place of unrivalled beauty — has terrific energy. It is also famous for wind, so be prepared.

Even tamed into a suburb, Gonzales Hill is an elemental place.

Just 20,000 years ago the whole area visible from here was covered in ice. Within about 5,000 years the ice was north of Gonzales Hill and melting fast. Imagine the passing of that glacier — the grinding and scraping, the waters pouring out.

Along the shore of Harling Point, just below the Chinese Cemetery, there are gneisses — hard metamorphosed rock — smooth as a

Michelangelo and creased like your best pants. The ice did that.

Within another 1,000 years, Gonzales Hill and most of Victoria was under water. A thousand years later the hill was a tiny peninsula with a forest of pines and alders.

The whole island rose as the weight of ice disappeared. By 10,000 years ago the shoreline was south of Trial Islands and the land swathed in Douglas fir grassland.

The dynamic of land and sea stabilized at the present level about 6000 years ago.

Details: *Gonzales Hill Regional Park: http://www.crd.bc.ca/parks/gonzales/index.htm. Downloadable map with directions.*
Geoscape Victoria, an informative geology website: http://geopanorama.rncan.gc.ca/victoria/index_e.php. Maps showing the history of deglaciation are under "The legacy of ice."

14   Oak Bay Islands

We live near a quiet corner of the Pacific Ocean. It takes 15 minutes to walk our self-propelled craft to the put-in by the Oak Bay Marina and be pulling away from shore. We leave familiar landscapes behind and enter a world of little islands with lively waters between.

The nearest island is Jimmy Chicken, five minutes from launch. It has a beautiful little beach edged with outcrops of polished gneisses. There's a 360° panorama from the rocky eminence. It's a good place to watch bald eagles and land-otters.

Jimmy Chicken and his wife Jenny were First Nations people who lived on the island before 1900 and legendarily sold seafood and crafted goods door to door.

Places here tend to have at least two names. The island's legal name is Mary Tod. Its old Salish name was *Kohweechella*, "where there are many fish." Regrettably, that is no longer the case.

Beyond the bay is a recreational wonderland. Considered among the best sailing anywhere — and extremely popular with whale watching boats — these waters get pretty choppy at times.

(In all my excursions I've never seen orca here — but a Gray whale sojourned in Oak Bay for two months in 2010.)

We next encounter some living museums of ecology.

The Oak Bay Islands Ecological Reserve is a protected archipelago with large gull and cormorant populations.

Ecological reserves are set aside for science and education. Public access is restricted to protect sensitive, rare and endangered ecosystems. Most are open to the public for no-impact hiking, birding and photography.

Because it has sensitive ecosystems, BC Parks requires visitors to get permission before visiting these islands. A few seabird colonies are closed to all but scientists.

A short paddle southwest brings us to Trial Islands Ecological Reserve. A refugium of plants that have been extirpated from the suburban waterfront, the reserve protects *the most outstanding known assemblage of rare and endangered plant species in British Columbia*. Permission is required to visit this botanical jewel, but you can make the highly scenic circumnavigation (1/2 hour) anytime conditions permit — just beware rips in the channel.

Eastward, we cross to the larger Discovery Islands, always with a weather eye. The tides flow through here at a clip — sometimes 6 or 7 knots past Strongtide Island, generating serious rips.

Winds can spring up and put you in sudden peril, and the smaller islands may not provide protection. Get a wind blowing against those rips, and you'll be fighting to keep the standing waves from flipping your boat.

You have an hour in this frigid water before hypothermia sets in — depending on your metabolic, emotional and physical reactions and how you are dressed.

We wait for slack tides and calm weather to cross.

Discovery Island Marine Park spans 2 km of the island's interesting south coast. There are good campsites in open meadows, but few facilities; no open fires.

The lighthouse at East Point dates from 1886. This, the third, is now automatic. All around are kelp beds. Seals are our constant companions.

The west half of Discovery Island and the two Chatham Islands belong to the Songhees First Nation. A group of Songhees people actually established a village on Discovery at the time of the 1862 smallpox epidemic.

The Chatham Islands are laced with channels challenging to navigate in currents.

To the east is Alpha Island, protected as part of Oak Bay Islands Ecological Reserve. This reserve protects rare plant communities. Permission required.

For the return crossing, we aim for Ten Mile Point. Mind you don't lag crossing in a flood tide and get swept through the passage.

Ten Mile Point Ecological Reserve is a subtidal area that is much studied as a benchmark for measuring change.

We're turning towards home now, with breaks to poke into interesting rocky coves and explore charming Flower Islet.

That's my neighbourhood — the wonders of nature 15 minutes from home.

Details: *Oak Bay Islands, Trial Islands, Ten Mile Point ecological reserves: http://www.env.gov.bc.ca/bcparks/eco_reserve/.*
Friends of Ecological Reserves : http://www.ecoreserves.bc.ca/.
Discovery Island Marine Provincial Park: http://www.env.gov.bc.ca/bcparks/explore/parkpgs/discovery_is/.
Discovery Island Lighthouse: http://www.discoveryisland.ca/.
Guided kayak tours of Oak Bay: Ocean River Sports, 5½-hour tours from Oak Bay Marina: http://www.oceanriver.com/day_tours.htm#explore.

Oak Bay House 15

The oldest house in Western Canada — the second oldest building in Victoria — was built in 1851 and is still at its original site on a charming property that retains the feel of a farm amid the suburban streets of Oak Bay.

"I was proposing to form a settlement between Point Gonzales and Cadboro point," James Douglas wrote to his Hudson's Bay Company superiors on September 1, 1850. It is "a part of the coast much frequented by the Natives [and acts] as an additional protection to the running stock; with that object in view . . . sold 100 acres of land to Chief Trader Tod, who is now living on the spot."

Wouldn't you know? — the first settler in Oak Bay, a district of famously ageing demographics, was a retiree.

John Tod (1794-1882) had a 40-year career with the HBC. While running the Thompson's River Post (Kamloops) he met his second wife, Sophia Lolo. I imagine they had a jolly time with their seven children on gorgeous Willows Farm.

The Estevan Ave shopping district has one of the city's notable restaurants, Paprika, and a fish and chip shop, Willows Galley.

A couple of outstanding parks are just a stone's throw away.

Scenic Willows Beach has a vibrant summertime scene and is much visited year-round. You might see a leathery old land-otter on the rocks near Cattle Point. For a few years a pair of bald eagles had a nest in a tall tree just above the rocks at the south end.

The rocky Garry oak woodland in 31-hectare Uplands Park gives a sense of the distinctive original ecosystem of the drier parts of the island.

Details: *John Tod House, 2564 Heron St, Oak Bay; much modified, the original shape obscured by additions; privately owned and occupied, so not accessible; Paprika Bistro: 2524 Estevan Ave, Oak Bay; (250 592-7424; http://www.paprika-bistro.com/. Willows Galley: 2559 Estevan Ave, Oak Bay; (250) 598-2711.*

16 Craigflower

Craigflower Manor is the distinctive white house with peaked windows near the west end of the Admirals Rd bridge. Built in 1853-56 by indentured workers of the Hudson's Bay Company, it was the centre of 364-hectare Craigflower Farm.

Across the bridge on Maple Point stands the original Craigflower School. Built in 1855, it is the oldest schoolhouse on its original site in Western Canada.

Both farmhouse and schoolhouse are National Historic Sites and among the oldest buildings on the island. They're open to the public seasonally, with interpretive programs depicting farm and school life in colonial times.

An ancient First Nations village stood near the sandy beach by the schoolhouse. Traces of habitat remain. Shell middens — garbage dumps, mostly of seafood — were analysed in a University of Victoria archaeology project. They revealed that the site was first occupied some 3,500 years ago.

At the time of European settlement, the Salish village of Kosapsom occupied Maple Point. The Kosapsom people sold their land to the Crown in 1854 and moved to a village on Esquimalt Harbour.

Craigflower itself dates from the first years of the colony of Vancouver Island. The HBC established four farms near Fort Victoria. Its subsidiary, the Puget Sound Agricultural Company, engaged hundreds of people to immigrate from the old country.

The staff of Craigflower, 37 families and 76 people, made the journey around Cape Horn and arrived at Fort Victoria in January 1853. They set to work clearing land, milling lumber and building the houses the HBC had told them were already built.

The workers poured their sweat into an enterprise named for the English estate of HBC governor Andrew Colvile. They were indentured for five years and paid £17 a year — one-quarter what they could earn as labourers on hire.

Desertions were only one of many problems that beset the HBC farms.

The bailiff (manager) of Craigflower was Kenneth McKenzie, who had managed the farms of his well-to-do family in Scotland. Many are the stories of bailiff McKenzie's challenges in the area of human relations.

Still, Craigflower was the least unsuccessful of the farms. McKenzie did well supplying the Royal Navy base with 1,000 lb of meat a day, all its vegetables and all the bakery goods — in purpose-built ovens, using Craigflower wheat.

The traffic on Admirals Rd went both ways. During the McKenzies' tenure, Craigflower was a party house for Naval society.

After the 1858 Gold Rush, the colony prospered, and the HBC soon wrote off its money-losing farms.

Craigflower was subdivided in 1866. The schoolhouse kept functioning until replaced in 1911.

The Admirals Rd bridge is identified locally with the murder of 14-year-old Reena Virk by bullying teens in 1997.

Details: *Craigflower Manor is at 110 Island Highway, View Royal and Craigflower Schoolhouse, 2765 Admirals Rd, Saanich.*
Craigflower National Historic sites are operating by The Land Conservancy of BC:

information, visiting times, directions: http://blog.conservancy.bc.ca/properties/
vancouver-island-region/craigflower-national-historic-sites-of-canada/
Teaching, Learning and Farming at Craigflower Farm, an educational website:
http://bcheritage.ca/craigflower/
Artifacts BC: a detailed account of archaeology at Kosapsom: http://bcheritage.
ca/artifacts/kosapsom/index.htm.

Fisgard Light and Esquimalt Harbour — 17

BC's first lighthouse, built 1860, stands at the entrance to Esquimalt Harbour, marking the rocks on the west shore. Accessible by land, Fisgard is the only functioning west coast lighthouse open to the public. Situated on a photogenic rocky islet, Fisgard Light has a spectacular prospect of the straits and approaches to Esquimalt Harbour.

The former lightkeeper's house has handsome exhibits of the technology of the day. The light was automated in 1929. Directly opposite the harbourmouth is Duntze Head, named after Captain John Duntze, master HM frigate *Fisgard*, 42 guns. *Fisgard* and other Royal Navy warships called in

TAKE 5 VANCOUVER ISLAND'S WARMEST PLACES

Places on the islands with the highest annual average daily temperature:

	° Celsius
1. **St Mary Lake, Salt Spring Island**	10.4
2. **Gonzales Heights, Oak Bay**	10.3 (tie)
Phyllis St, Victoria	
3. **Cortes Island**	10.2 (tie)
Departure Bay, Nanaimo	
Mayne Island	
4. **William Head, Metchosin**	10.1
5. **Islandview, Central Saanich**	10.0

From Environment Canada's Canadian Climate Normals 1971-2000 *(climate.weatheroffice.gc.ca).*

Places with the highest annual average daily temperatures in Canada:

Vancouver, BC (Harbour)	11.0
Chilliwack, BC	10.5 (tie)
White Rock, BC	

there during the first years of Fort Victoria.

Esquimalt Harbour is spacious and deep with a defensible entrance and as a result the Royal Navy established a presence here. Their presence help dull the American appetite for ever more land. The 1844 American election slogan "54-40 or fight" summarized the US claim to possess the entire northwest coast to Alaska (54°40' N latitude).

At least 43 warships and gunboats were stationed here during the first decades of the colony. They're listed in Colin Browne's poem *Diplomacy, Vancouver Island, 1845-1865*.

The Fisgard light was the first permanent construction around the naval precinct. By 1864 a functioning naval yard was established in the lee of Duntze Head. It became the Royal Navy's Pacific Station — squadron headquarters — in 1865. Today it is still known as HMC Dockyard, and it is the heart of Canadian Forces Base Esquimalt.

On the south side of Duntze Head, well-cultivated waterfront property surrounds the 1885 red brick Admiral's House. A number of heritage buildings from that period survive in Dockyard.

By BC's terms of union, Canada agreed to build a drydock in Esquimalt Harbour. After much delay it was completed in 1887. The drydock was of vital use for Royal Navy vessels in the North Pacific. It was used until a much larger drydock was built across the harbour in the 1920s.

The harbour's strategic value increased with the establishment of an Admiralty coaling station — the only one in the eastern Pacific — supplied by Nanaimo coal.

Pacific Station became a likely target for seizure by foreign navies. In 1877 England and Russia were rattling sabres. Russia's Pacific naval base at Vladivostok was heavily armed.

The war scare resulted in construction of the first shoreline batteries of heavy guns along the Victoria waterfront.

Fort Rodd Hill, constructed in the 1890s above Fisgard Light at the entrance of the harbour, was the culminating fortification. The battery was in service until the 1950s. During World War II it was the headquarters of an elaborate system of sea-lane surveillance, with lookouts posted on prominences from East Sooke to Oak Bay.

The Royal Navy maintained the Esquimalt base until 1905. A five-year hiatus ensued before the Canadian Navy took possession in 1910.

CFB Esquimalt celebrated the base's centenary in 2010. Fisgard Light marks 150 years of service on November 16, 2010.

They stand on guard for the community their presence did much to shape.

Details: *Fisgard Lighthouse National Historic Site: http://www.fisgardlighthouse.com. Fort Rodd Hill National Historic Site: http://www.fortroddhill.com. Entrance to both is via Ocean Blvd, Colwood. CFB Esquimalt, seasonal tours of Dockyard and Naden: (250) 363-5291, www. cfbesquimalt.ca.*

18   The Galloping Goose and Lochside Trails

The Galloping Goose and Lochside Regional Trails are among Victoria's best loved amenities.

Four railways once served Victoria. Of the three that didn't survive, one became Interurban Road and two have been recycled as multi-use trails.

The 29-km Lochside follows old railbeds between Victoria and North Saanich en route to BC Ferries' Swartz Bay terminal. Much closer to the city, it passes the delightful Swan Lake Christmas Hill Nature Sanctuary (Km 5). This 58-ha urban preserve, a Saanich municipal park, has a 2.5-km circuit of the quiet lake and a hike to a rocky summit with 360° views of the city. (The nature house also has terrific programs.)

The Galloping Goose uses 55 km of railbed on a line that ran west to Sooke and north to Cowichan Lake. The original Galloping Goose was a self-propelled railcar that provided daily passenger service between Victoria, Milnes Landing (Sooke), West Shawnigan Lake and Cowichan Lake, 1924-31.

For a longer biking day-trip passing through increasingly rural landscapes, we would choose from two rides on the Goose.

The nearer route begins at Atkins Rd and winds through Victoria's Western Communities en route to Sooke. We drive (or bus) to the Atkins Road parking lot, near Km 10, in Colwood to avoid the haul from downtown and a stretch along Highway 1.

(A friendlier route to the Atkins Rd parking lot is under construction — the E&N Rail Trail between downtown Victoria and Langford.)

Metchosin is particularly scenic, with small farms and four exquisite regional parks at Witty's Lagoon, Devonian Beach, Matheson Lake and Roche Cove. Round trip to Roche Cove: 50 km.

The farther route begins near Roche Cove. Drive or bus the Sooke Road to Gillespie Road. West from Roche Cove (Km 35) the trail follows Sooke Harbour, then climbs into the Sooke Hills, past the Sooke Potholes (Km 48) to the terminus at Leechtown (Km 55). There are long inclines and some challenging crossings. Round trip: 40 km.

The low grades and smooth roadbeds of our linear parks are a gift from the past.

Details: *Maps, directions and descriptions of the Lochside and Galloping Goose trails and regional parks in Metchosin at Capital Regional Parks: www.crd.bc.ca/ parks. For Swan Lake Christmas Hill Nature Sanctuary: swanlake.bc.ca. (Note: no biking or dogs allowed.)*
E&N Rail Trail: http://www.crd.bc.ca/parks/e_n_railtrail.htm.

The Butchart Gardens 19

In the City of Gardens, the Butchart Gardens is the centrepiece. The famous 22-hectare show garden, on an estate near Brentwood Bay, displays nature at its gaudiest. It's one of the city's premier attractions, so solitude is usually not part of the experience.

I have been to Butchart's many times, in all seasons, in daylight and at dusk, and taken many visitors there. Pressed to name a favorite spot, I choose the Rose Garden, beautifully sited on an open slope with benches near a curious spherical mirror.

The fireworks display, Saturday evenings in the summer, is not to be missed. You can take a picnic basket and sit on the grass. (If you forget blankets, they sell them.) The fireworks are the old-fashioned kind, with pinwheels and lines of little displays, their firings perfectly matched to a suite of contemporary music. Viewed against the silhouettes of the nearby mountains, they are enchanting.

The Butchart family was prominent in the cement business. They moved to Tod Inlet from Ontario and built the handsome house in 1904. What is now the Sunken Garden was once a limestone quarry.

Mrs Butchart hired some noted landscape architects to design the gardens. After the quarry was exhausted she set to work landscaping it. By the 1920s Mrs Butchart ran a flourishing mail-order seed business, and the gardens were attracting 50,000 visitors a year. Today, after more than 100 years the property, still in the family, is a National Historic Site.

Details: *The Butchart Gardens, 800 Benvenuto Ave, Brentwood Bay (23 km north of Victoria), (250) 652-5256; open year round: http://www.butchartgardens.com.*

20 Sidney, Booktown

Sidney, the sunny seaside settlement north of Victoria, styles itself a *booktown*, the centre of which would be Tanner's Books at Beacon and Fourth. It's a place to explore, with a stock of trade books, magazines, newspapers and nautical charts. A bit west is Beacon Books, an arcadia of old books, magazines, pictures, postcards and paper ephemera. Both have great local sections, and they always stock my book *The Story of Sidney*, God bless em.

In a centre of books, can writers be far away? The presiding spirit would be Al Purdy (1918-2000), icon of Canadian poets of the two-fisted variety. Purdy lived half the year in Sidney with his wife Eurithe, who he referred to at a Victoria poetry reading as "the woman who keeps me in the manner to which I have become accustomed." He was wearing a raincoat and a toque.

We call Purdy ours — he wasn't really. The search for winter warmth brought them here. Purdy died in Sidney, but his ashes were scattered around their property in Ameliasburg, Ontario, where their famous A-Frame house is.

Across the narrow Saanich Peninsula is a noted alliance of authors who pair up like this: Susan Musgrave and Stephen Reid, Patrick Lane and Lorna Crozier.

Susan Musgrave is a poet of local nurture who in the course of publishing more than 25 books of poems and prose has cultivated an eccentric, ironic persona that is extravagantly expressed in her automobile. It is completely covered with molded plastic figures. Her most recent book was *When the World is Not Our Home: Selected Poems 1985-2000* (Thistledown, 2009).

Writing doesn't get much grittier than Stephen Reid's. His contribution to a 2005 *Book of Lists:* the toughest prisons in North America, first-hand.

Musgrave and Reid live part-time on Haida Gwaii.

Patrick Lane's first novel, *Red Dog, Red Dog*, was published in 2008 to critical acclaim. He began writing with serious intent in 1960, his website attests.

Lorna Crozier's most recent book was a memoir of Saskatchewan, *Small Beneath the Sky* (2009).

Both poets have won Governor General's Awards for Literary Excellence, and both have been chair of the writing department at the University of Victoria.

Details: *Sidney Booktown: 9 places on Google Maps (maps.google.com).*
Tanner's Books: 2436 Beacon Avenue.
Beacon Books: 2372 Beacon Avenue.
Susan Musgrave: http://www.susanmusgrave.com/.
Patrick Lane: http://www.patricklane.ca/.
Lorna Crozier: http://www.lornacrozier.ca/.
Stephen Reid's 10 toughest prisons in North America: http://www.macleans.ca/ culture/books/article.jsp?content=20051222_140126_5452.

Goldstream   21

Goldstream Provincial Park protects 477 hectares of incredibly varied terrain around the narrow defile of Goldstream River, 26 kilometres west of downtown Victoria. Goldstream is particularly famous for its fall salmon run, the most accessible on the island. (It's literally right beside Highway 1.)

Trails wind through the park's enchanting old-growth forest of mostly Douglas firs. Among the trails is one of the oldest on the island. The original up-island trail (built in 1861) followed the upper Goldstream en route to Shawnigan Lake.

From Goldstream you can climb a trail beside the waterfall of the Niagara River to the 1886 iron trestle of the Esquimalt & Nanaimo Railway. The trestle is more than 80 metres above the floor of the canyon. (Watch for trains!)

Mt Finlayson, 419 m elevation, is the highest point in the Victoria area, with great views in three directions. The trail up Mt Finlayson starts near the river and is a locals' favorite — challenging, with some steep bits and some scrambling over smooth rock. The west face has dangerous cliffs.

The park's main attraction is undoubtedly the annual run of Chum salmon in Goldstream River. The fish spawn near the mouth of the little river starting in October. It is the stage for a poignant drama of nature.

Set amid a coniferous forest with large western redcedar trees, the riparian zone is a busy place in the fall. The fish make their way upstream in search of gravel, where they mate in that strange no-contact way, females and males depositing in turn their eggs and milt. Their mottled remains become objects of competition among gulls and eagles and myriad other feeders — the food chain is wide here.

Viewing the pageant of death and new life, one contemplates the gift of the migrating salmon. This run is repeated in countless rivers, some far from tidewater, for six oceangoing species of Pacific salmon.

A nature house, busy on fall weekends and holidays, sits just above the estuary at the head of Finlayson Arm. On the front porch, kids paint fresh salmon carcasses and press sheets of paper over them to imprint the coloured contours of the fish.

This highly scenic spot overlooks, to the north, one of Victoria's most interesting landscapes, across the estuary and down the narrow, steep-walled fjord.

Goldstream Park has one of the island's most popular campgrounds.

Details: *Goldstream Provincial Park: http://www.env.gov.bc.ca/bcparks/explore/ parkpgs/goldstream/.*

22 — East Sooke and Race Rocks

Peninsular East Sooke is a rural enclave with one tiny through-road and some amazing dead-ends. East Sooke Park, a 1,434-hectare slice of it, provides a taste of the wild west coast within an hour of downtown Victoria.

The rugged 10-kilometre coast trail between the Aylard Farm and Pike Pt is a full day's hike one-way. The coast is rocky and highly scenic, with windswept forests of pine, fir, spruce and cedar. From many prominences there are spectacular views across the Strait of Juan de Fuca.

The network of interior trails is notable for climbs up Mount Maguire and Babbington Hill. They're best begun at Anderson Cove.

For briefer excursions, the Aylard Farm area is full of pleasures. The short walk to Creyke Pt. leads to exhilarating views across Becher Bay. The waterfront petroglyphs at Alldridge Point is less than half an hour one-way. There's a 20-million-year-old beach of conglomerate. The lookout at Beechey Head is less than an hour.

Race Rocks is a tiny islet and the surrounding reefs 1.5 km southeast of Christopher Point. It is the southernmost point in British Columbia. The Race Rocks light has warned ships off the rocks since 1860 — it came into service days after the Fisgard light.

Race Rocks' high-current channels support abundant sea-life that is attractive to feeding sea mammals. Two species of sea lions gather by the hundreds on the rocks in winter. Enormous sea elephants breed there. Orcas often visit in summer. It's an internationally known marine biology research site.

Protected as an ecological reserve since 1980, and a marine protected area besides, Race Rocks is under the watchful eye of Pearson College, a prestigious United World College in nearby Pedder Bay.

Marine science students at Pearson are the volunteer wardens of the ecological reserve. They study changes in the ecosystem and run an experimental installation that uses current to generate electricity. They keep a detailed website chronicling their interventions.

The college employs the lightkeepers. Try to land without a permit and you will quickly be shoo'd away. No permit? You can watch and listen to the wildlife at Race Rocks real-time through a cam on the college website.

Pearson College sponsors occasional field trips to the reserve, which I highly recommend. It's an elemental place, and the advanced work of the high-school diver-researchers is amazing.

Details: *East Sooke is accessible via Gillespie Rd, off the Sooke Rd (Highway 14) or by East Sooke Rd, of Rocky Point Rd, Metchosin.*
East Sooke Regional Park: http://www.crd.bc.ca/parks/eastsooke/.
Main points of access: Aylard Farm, end of Becher Bay Rd; Anderson Cove and Pike Rd, both on E Sooke Rd.
Pearson College Race Rocks website: http://www.racerocks.com/.
Lester B. Pearson College of the Pacific is off Rocky Point Rd in Metchosin: http://www.pearsoncollege.ca/. Casual visitors are welcome to explore the 30-ha waterfront campus of the 2-year full-scholarship baccalaureate preparatory school.

Sooke Harbour House   23

The dining room of this country inn continues to appear on lists of Canada's best restaurants. For some it is the very fountainhead of slow food culture on the island. Sooke Harbour House is also a destination whose centerpiece is a charming old house with the bounties of nature at the door, spectacularly located on Juan de Fuca Strait, just where the west coast begins to catch the flavour of the open Pacific.

Sooke Harbour House's gardens and farm grow every possible edible thing for use in the kitchen. After all, this is the only area in Canada where extremely high-quality ingredients are available year 'round. The restaurant serves a greater variety of foods than most, yet the menu is completely a reflection of the area — indeed, it has helped to revive local, independent agriculture. Everything is served in season.

The emphasis on fresh, local, organic foods may be commonplace now. In the 1980s, however, Sooke Harbour House was a pioneer. This culinary Mecca began so modestly, cooking was actually an afterthought.

Sinclair Philip grew up in Alberta and spent summers with his parents on the east side of Vancouver Island. Usually they stayed at the Oyster River Cottages, south of Campbell River. They rented little fishing boats and cooked the catch in the cottage. Frederique Philip is from France. They met at a party in Nice when Sinclair was living in France. Both had trained as economists.

When they evolved the idea of a waterfront resort, the Philips looked for the kind of place Sinclair remembered. On the east side of the island there was no such place — that they could afford. The west coast was much less visited. And Sooke Harbour House was in their range.

The place has had that name since 1929. They re-opened it in 1979 on a shoestring, serving food to make ends meet. The southern exposure made it a good place for year-round business. They began to attract visitors from Vancouver and Seattle. Many wanted lighter, healthier food. The cuisine became more elaborate and sophisticated.

As the cachet of the west coast grew, so did the reputation of Sooke Harbour House. Several additions and renovations later, it is a 28-room luxury resort with meeting rooms and a spa. An art gallery shows the work of Vancouver Island artists.

Reservations are a must for dinner. The menu changes every day. If you want to sample the cuisine and ambience, try the three-course special dinner ($45). Lunch is served on Sundays.

Be sure to leave time for a walk to the end of Whiffen Spit to absorb the views of Sooke Harbour, East Sooke and the straits.

Details: *Sooke Harbour House, 1528 Whiffen Spit Rd, Sooke, is a 45-60-minute drive from Victoria; 1-800-889-9688, (250) 642-3421; sookeharbourhouse.com.*

24 Sooke Potholes

The Sooke River is the second largest river on southern Vancouver Island, draining an area of nearly 28,000 hectares west of Victoria. A lot of water hits the bluish rocks of the Sooke Hills. The cool, clear water tumbles through fluted galleries, falls into black pools and flattens into ponds with gravelly beaches.

These are the famous Sooke Potholes that have delighted generations of swimmers. As a kid, my favorite place in the world was the Potholes. On a hot day, watch them fill up with grateful swimmers of all ages.

Sooke Potholes Regional Park protects an 8.5-kilometre-long stretch of the river. There's pay parking and some facilities. A gorgeous 65-site campground fronts the river at the north end of the park. Operated seasonally by the Land Conservancy of BC (TLC), it has many reservable sites.

The real story here is about the endlessly beautiful rock formations. It looks like the river must have been carving the hard, hard rock for millions of years. In fact, geologists believe the potholes were formed about 15,000 years ago.

The rock itself is basalt and has been dated to between 55.8 and 33.9 million years ago. It began on the ocean floor, where molten magma squirts or oozes out and instantly solidifies. It built up into seamounts and islands, becoming part of what geologists call the Metchosin Igneous Complex.

Now the story gets interesting. Earth's crust comprises a few big continent-sized plates and many small terranes that float on a molten mantle and move around, pushed by seafloor spreading — so goes the theory of plate tectonics.

Seafloor spreading pushed the Crescent Terrane, bearing those basalts, northward. The leading edge of the terrane apparently subducted — got pushed under — older rock. Eventually it ground to a halt. Behind it, however, seafloor spreading seems to have continued to push the terrane north. The basalts of the Metchosin Igneous Complex had only one way to go — up. They were uplifted.

A mere 15,000 years ago, kilometer-high ice blanketed most of the island, but when it began to disappear, meltwater poured out of the hollowing glacier. Torrents of water — full of boulders, rocks, gravel, sand — descended in a thundering vortex, scraping and scouring away at the rock, creating one of the island's most enchanting landscapes.

Details: *Information, map, directions to Sooke Potholes Regional Park: www.crd. bc.ca/parks. For information about the Sooke Potholes campground and to make reservations through TLC: blog.conservancy.bc.ca/ecotourism.*
Geological History of Vancouver Island: an overview with links to more detailed information: http://www.crd.bc.ca/watersheds/protection/geology-processes/ geologicalhistoryVI.htm.

Leechtown   25

Leechtown is the western terminus of the Galloping Goose Regional Trail — a mixture of forest, brush and open meadow at the juncture of the Sooke and Leech rivers. There's not much to see — an old plaque, a display. What's the deal? It's hard to believe now, but there once was a town or two here.

Before European settlement, the area was crossed by trails. The T'Sou-ke First Nation traveled on them between Sooke, Saanich and Cowichan.

In 1864 a party of 10 explorers, plus two guide-hunters and a few hangers-on, crisscrossed the island, surveying its natural resources and noting their use by indigenous peoples. The expedition's instructions, however, were to find mineral bodies. A prize of £1,000 had been put up for "the discovery of paying gold fields."

Leader Robert Brown related how "on 26th July, the whole party arrived, having, as I expected, found gold on a tributary of Sooke river, which we named Leech river, and which no white man . . . had previously reached."

The reports caused a sensation in Victoria. A thousand would-be miners rushed into the Sooke Hills. Leechtown quickly had stores, hotels and saloons. The Leech did not live up to high hopes, and the rush petered out within a year — although by 1876, it was estimated, $100,000 worth of gold had been recovered. Any time the price of gold rises, prospectors still turn out.

Today, hardly a trace survives of Leechtown, Boulder City, Kennedy Flats or Thompsons Landing.

After mining came logging. In the 1920s the Victoria-Cowichan railway line opened the area's forests. Kapoor Lumber, owned by Kapoor Singh Siddoo and Mayo Singh, Sikh immigrants, built an Indo-Canadian forest empire that included the area. The Cameron Lumber Company built a sawmill near Leechtown. Workers' families moved into the little settlement.

That was long ago. As happens around the island, logging has given way to recreation.

In 1999, the Capital Regional District acquired 1,300 hectares of Kapoor lands through a land swap. The purpose was to provide a security buffer around the reservoir where Victoria gets most of its drinking water.

The Kapoor family also donated 13 hectares of land at Leechtown, between the railbed and the Sooke River, for a CRD park.

Bill Irvine's father worked as a carpenter at Kapoor Lumber in the 20s and he has a flickr photostream with photos and detailed notes of his regular visits as well as a walking blog. He considers Leechtown "a marvelous place." He always tries to get down to the Deep Pool at the confluence of the Sooke and Leech rivers. You should too.

Details: *Robert Brown's 28-page narrative,* Vancouver Island: Exploration, 1864 *can be read on Google Books (books.google.ca).*
Bill Irvine's photostream: www.flickr.com/photos/wjis21; and his blog: wjiwalks. blogspot.com.
CRD Kapoor park reserve: http://www.crd.bc.ca/parks/reserves/kapoor.htm.

Southeast Vancouver Island and the Gulf Islands

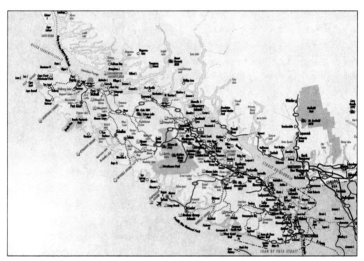

Southeast Vancouver Island is on the dry side of the mountain spine, facing the Strait of Georgia and taking in the Gulf Islands. More than 300,000 people live along the sunny, scenic coastal margin between the Cowichan and Comox valleys, including fast-growing residential enclaves around Duncan, Nanaimo, Parksville-Qualicum and Courtenay-Comox. These traditional lands of Salish First Nations became the base for the island's first industry, coal mining, while the heartland of the Douglas fir forest supported logging, sawmilling, pulp and paper industries. Today the warm lands of the southeast island nurture heritage farms and vineyards off bucolic back roads. Nearby and yet a world apart are the Gulf Islands, a mariner's paradise by sea, by land the gourmandiser's happy hunting ground.

26   Malahat Lookouts

If you're driving up-island from Victoria, you pretty much have to use The Malahat, a mountainous, at times scenic 25 kilometres of Highway 1. From the sea-level canyon of Goldstream the road climbs to a 352-metre summit as it winds across the face of Malahat Ridge.

Two lookouts provide spectacular views of Saanich Inlet and a respite from the traffic. If visibility is good, the views are not to be missed. (The lookouts are, however, accessible only from the northbound lane.)

The first stop, about 10 km from Goldstream, looks south toward Finlayson Arm. The tapering body of water, edged by walls of rock, is the head of a fjord — the only one on the north side of the island. Opposite Malahat Ridge is the rugged expanse known as the Highlands, dominated by Mt Finlayson. Much of the Highlands bordering Finlayson Arm is protected in Gowlland-Tod Provincial Park; beyond, the rolling green of Victoria's western borders is framed by the distant Olympic Mountains.

The second lookout, about 3 kms further, provides gorgeous vistas to the east and north. Across Saanich Inlet lies the mostly agricultural Saanich Peninsula, a verdant greenspace broken by the suburb of Brentwood Bay and the forested slopes of Mt Newton. Further east lie the American San Juan islands, with snow-capped Mt Baker beyond. The Canadian Gulf Islands are sometimes framed by the Coast Mountains, north of Vancouver.

At this rock-bound spot it's possible to visualize what the original Malahat Drive was like. Completed in 1911 after decades of work, the first tiny road was a hair-raising adventure. The lookout preserves a fragment of the original route. Just imagine it without railings.

The Brentwood Bay-Mill Bay ferry plies Saanich Inlet and provides a link with the Malahat for those who enjoy making a circuit. Some bound for Victoria from up-island prefer the more leisurely ferry route to driving the busy Malahat.

Details: *Current road conditions on the Malahat: images.drivebc.ca/bchighwaycam. Brentwood Bay-Mill Bay ferry: www.bcferries.com. The 3 km crossing costs about $40 for car and driver; cash/travellers' cheques only.*

Shawnigan Lake   27

Shawnigan Lake is a lovely summer resort nestled in rollercoaster foothills. Historic East Shawnigan Lake Road, originally a trail blazed in 1861, winds past cottages and docks and through the village.

Below the village, the Esquimalt and Nanaimo Railway (E&N) track skirts the shore. Twice daily a railcar stops at the shelter. The E&N's continued passenger service turns on a point of history — the land grant that went with the railway carried an obligation to keep it running.

The E&N was once of vital importance to the island's development. At Cliffside, a whistle stop 4 kilometres south of the village, there's a cairn commemorating the inauguration of the 116-km railway. On August

TAKE 5 JOHN SCHREINER'S FIVE
FAVORITE ISLAND WINERIES

Author of *The Wineries of British Columbia* (3rd edition 2009) and 13 other books on wine, John Schreiner keeps a blog, *John Schreiner on Wine* (http://johnschreiner.blogspot.com/) and publishes articles in numerous periodicals. A native of Saskatchewan, he was a career business writer with *The Financial Post*. He lives in North Vancouver, BC.

Winemaking in British Columbia began with the making of berry wines on Vancouver Island in the 1920s. The modern era of island winemaking began in 1992 with the opening of Vigneti Zanatta. Since then about 35 wineries have been established, making everything from berry and grape wines to cider and mead. Here are my favorites.

1. **Averill Creek Vineyard**, 6552 North Rd., Duncan, (250) 709-9986.
Grape grower and former doctor Andy Johnston offers fine Pinot Noir and Pinot Gris in the Cowichan Valley's most elegant tasting room.

2. **Beaufort Vineyard and Estate Winery**, 5854 Pickering Rd., Courtenay, (250) 338-1357.
Wine growers Jeff and Susan Vandermolen settled there in 2005 after a travel-filled oil industry career, including navigating a sailboat across the Atlantic. A replica of an Easter Island Moai, carved from cedar, stares blindly over the vineyard toward the distant Beaufort Mountains.

3. **Garry Oaks Winery**, 1880 Fulford-Ganges Rd., Salt Spring Island, (250) 653-4687.
Produces excellent wines from a picturesque vineyard that includes a maze. The bonus for island visitors is the bucolic picnic spot at the winery next door, Salt Spring Vineyards, 151 Lee Rd at 1700 block Fulford-Ganges Rd, (250) 653-9463.

4. **Starling Lane Winery**, 5271 Old West Saanich Rd., Saanich, (250) 881-7422.
Has its tasting room in the garden-like setting of a heritage farm, a popular wedding venue. Elegant Ortega and Pinot Gris are hand-crafted by winemaker and partner John Wrinch, a Victoria radiologist.

5. **Venturi-Schulze Vineyards**, 4235 Vineyard Rd, Cobble Hill, (250) 743-5630.
Notable for creative wines (great sparkling, Pinot Noir and dry whites) and balsamic vinegar true in style to those of Modena, where winemaker Giordano Venturi was born.

13, 1886 the Prime Minister of Canada, Sir John A. Macdonald — Mister National Dream himself — hammered in the E&N's last spike, made of gold. With that the hinterland of the island's richly endowed southeastern quarter opened for business — the 8,000 sq km that was given to coal magnate Robert Dunsmuir as an incentive to build the line.

One km south of the village, where the tracks curve away from the shore, is 7-hectare Old Mill Park. Pathways wind through a lacustrine landscape shaded by mostly deciduous forest. There's a viewing platform on the shore. It's a good place to see waterfowl, sunsets and the old dophins of the Shawnigan Lake Lumber Company.

Shawnigan Lake had one of the first sawmills along the E&N, built by the Losee family in 1890. The company changed hands several times, and the mill burned down three times. Twice the enterprise bounced back, and the owners were always able to buy more timber west of Shawnigan Lake.

The mill became a mainstay of the local economy. In its peak years in the 1920s, it employed 150 workers and another 100 in the woods. Geared locomotives brought logs down the slopes and onto a long wooden trestle where West Shawnigan Lake Park is today. The logs were dumped into the lake, to be towed to the mill by steam tugs. The finished lumber was loaded onto E&N railcars and off to market.

In 1942, Vancouver's budding industrial magnate H.R. MacMillan bought the Shawnigan Lake Lumber Company. He needed timber for his much bigger sawmills. He soon considered the mill not worth fixing up and shut it down.

Favoured by nature, Shawnigan Lake survived on seasonal tourism and recreation. The first hotel, long-gone Morton House, opened in 1885. There has been a succession of resorts ever since. The Strathcona Hotel, built in 1900 (twice), went bust in the 1920s and was for decades a girls' private school.

In the 50s it was an adventure to drive up The Malahat. Shawnigan Lake was appealingly remote from Victoria. Enclosed by second-growth forest, it certainly wasn't peaceful, with speedboats and float planes buzzing up and down in summer.

Shawnigan Lake is starting to become a bedroom community, with large back lots and more than its share of greenspace. The lake retains its charm, and at Old Mill Park the human past glints through the world of nature.

Details: *Information about Old Mill Park (access, facilities, map) under community parks at www.cvrd.bc.ca. Parking lot off Recreation Rd, W of Shawnigan Lake Rd.*
E&N passenger service between Victoria and Courtenay (225 km): www.viarail.ca.

28 Kinsol Trestle

This towering wooden construction, 44 metres high and 188 m long, spans the Koksilah River near Shawnigan Lake. Wooden railway trestles were once common on the island, built to traverse its many carved river valleys. The Bear Creek trestle was 76 m high and Haslam Creek, 60 m.

The trestles disappeared with the railways. Today the Kinsol is the largest remaining Howe truss pile-bent trestle and is believed to be one of largest wooden structures anywhere.

The long-abandoned bridge was until recently a wreck — hazardous and closed to public use. We could only gaze at the massive ruins. A construction team has been hard at work on the Kinsol Trestle. A local campaign has been fund-raising to match pledges by governments and the Trans Canada Trail society. The restoration, estimated to cost $7.5 million, is expected to be completed by Summer 2011.

With a solid deck and railings, the trestle will become part of the 22,000-kilometre-long Trans Canada Trail. Once again it will provide vital linkage.

Construction of a railbed from Victoria to Port Alberni began in 1911 as part of the Canadian Northern Pacific Railway. Local farmers and loggers furnished the labour, but little track was laid.

The Esquimalt & Nanaimo Railway had completed a branch line to Cowichan Lake in 1913. The railway jump-started the logging industry there. CNR's Cowichan Lake line cashed in on the boom.

The Kinsol Trestle, completed in 1920, was a vital link in the Cowichan line. It took the name of the train station near the short-lived King Solomon mine. The gas-powered Galloping Goose passenger car started operating from Victoria as far as Milnes Landing in 1922, to Lake Cowichan in 1924 and the following year to Youbou. The service lasted only until 1931.

Logging companies started operating near the line. The logs went to Cowichan Bay tidewater on a CNR spur line. The Cowichan line continued to serve the logging industry until the 50s.

The last train rolled across the Kinsol Trestle in 1979.

The Trans-Canada Trail uses the old CN grade between Sooke Lake Road and Lake Cowichan. At the south terminus, there's parking off Sooke Lake Road. The restored trail proceeds along the west side of Shawnigan Lake 13 kms to the Kinsol Trestle detour.

The trail continues into the Cowichan River Valley to Lake Cowichan and is well-maintained.

At Deerholme, it meets the 17-km right of way from the Cowichan estuary. Known as the Tidewater Railtrail, the route is kept clear by residents.

Details: *Directions to the north end of the Kinsol Trestle: Trans-Canada Highway to Koksilah Rd heading W; L on Riverside Rd just past Koksilah River bridge; at 8.5* *km, parking on L; 5-minute walk. To the south end: From the Village of Shawnigan Lake, follow Renfrew Road W; R on Glen Eagles Rd, R on Shelby Rd; parking area on L; follow Trans Canada Trail N.*

More about the Kinsol Trestle and the capital campaign to restore it: www.kinsol.ca.

Map and description of the Cowichan section of the Trans Canada Trail: on Cowichan Valley Regional District website (www.cvrd.bc.ca) find Cowichan Valley Trail under regional parks.

Merridale Estate Cidery 29

Merridale Cidery entices a stream of customers to the countryside of Cobble Hill, offering the experience, almost unique in North America, of English-style dry ciders, made on the premises with apples from the orchard. The apples are heritage old-country cider-making varieties. Unlike eating or dessert apples, they have high tannin content, like wine grapes, and are therefore quite acidic. Merridale's splendid website has detailed notes on the varieties and processes it employs.

The time-tested techniques practiced in the ciderworks, which can be toured during working hours, include *fermenting to dry*, to take out the sugars. The result is "a heck of a lot different," says co-proprietor Janet Docherty, "from what we were used to in BC."

Our neighbours Jim and Dawn drive up to Merridale for lunch occasionally. In his youth on a farm near Creston, Jim tried to make cider with eating apples. "It was never anything like this." He considers the dry ciders comparable to wine as an accompaniment to food. Jim especially likes the strong Somerset cider.

BC's first estate cidery began under the previous owner, with plantings of cider apples from England, France and Germany. Cobble Hill was chosen for its growing conditions — a microclimate that has, Docherty says, "a tremendous amount of sunshine but is usually not too hot or too cold."

Docherty and husband Rick Pipes purchased the cidery in 2000. They knew nothing about cider but — business graduates both, with a family — were looking for a investment that involved a healthy lifestyle. From their serendipitous discovery of Merrridale, the vision evolved of an agricultural operation people would want to visit.

There is a spacious tasting room and a restaurant, Bistro la Pommeraie, that features local ingredients and tends to the creative. Visitors can also tour the orchard. Merridale recently added a distillery for making apple brandy.

Merridale limits distribution of the eight ciders, four eaus de vie, apple juice and cider vinegar, so there's another inducement to go there.

Do read the Cider House Rules. It's all there — "Always designate a driver to get you home safely."

Details: *Merridale Estate Cidery, 1230 Merridale Road, Cobble Hill, (250) 743-4293; merridalecider.com.*

30 | Mt Tzouhalem

Mt Tzouhalem is the rampart of rock on the north side of Cowichan Bay. A white cross, visible from across the bay, stands at the edge of a cliff a few hundred metres short of the 536-metre-high summit of Mt Tzouhalem. It's an hour's easy climb through forest to the cross.

What you find there is a little grassy knoll sheltered by outcrops of knobby conglomerate, a Garry Oak tree ringed by red-barked arbutus trees in the middle and manzanita bushes at the fringes. It overlooks the Cowichan Valley and is an excellent place to get the lie of the land. The panoramic view in three directions is simply breathtaking.

Far to the west, over a ridge, is Cowichan Lake. The lake is 31 kilometres long, and from its outlet the Cowichan River flows east on a 47-km path to tidewater while dropping 164 metres. The narrow valley opens onto a floodplain.

You see the Cowichan River as it flows through the city of Duncan, picking up the tributary watersheds of Quamichan and Somenos lakes — visible past Tzouhalem's western flank — and, near its mouth, joined by the Koksilah River, which drains the other side of the valley. The rivers meet salt water in an estuary 2.5 km wide and 1 km deep.

This is the richly fertile land Hul'q'umi'num-speaking Salish peoples have owned and occupied "since time immemorial" and never surrendered.

First Nations didn't have a name for the whole valley, but the traditional name of the Mt Tzouhalem is *Shquw'utsun* (Cowichan), meaning "a giant frog who lay on his side basking in the warm sun." The mountain is an important setting in the First People's creation myths.

Beginning in the 1850s the valley was settled by European farmers, after its agricultural potential was advertised by the Hudson's Bay Company.

The Europeans appropriated the name Cowichan, using it for the entire valley. They gave the word a new twist of meaning — "the warm land."

The settlers gave the mountain a new name as well. *Ts'uwxxilem* (Tzouhalem) was an historical resident of the valley whose violent way of collecting wives became legendary. *Ts'uwxxilem* had lived with his wives in a stronghold at the base of the mountain. That may account for the use of his name. His violence was an object of deep fear and loathing in some First Nations families. In others, his strong medicine excites great reverence even today.

In the book *Two Houses Half-Buried in Sand* by Chris Arnett (2007) there's a narrative of *Ts'uwxxilem* acquiring spiritual powers. Supernatural events occurred on Cowichan Mountain/Mt Tzouhalem. It's a gripping tale.

You certainly get a long view from Mt Tzouhalem.

Details: *Mt Tzouhalem's western slope can easily be climbed by road and trail from the gravel parking lot just south of St Ann's Church, 1775 Tzouhalem Rd. The trail is unmarked, and much of the mountain is criss-crossed with bike trails and logging roads — it's both a working municipal forest and a popular mountain biking destination. Best make a first climb with someone who knows the route.*

The east side of Mt Tzouhalem can be hiked by a trail that begins near the end of Khenipsen Road.

Providence Farm 31

This working organic farm, nestled under Mt Tzouhalem, is the centre of a therapeutic community "dedicated to restoring the spirit and skills of those with physical, mental and emotional challenges." Providence is what is called a *care farm* or *social farm*. There are few in Canada, but perhaps 1,000 in Europe, where it is a real genuine movement. I'd say Providence Farm is worth a special trip.

The farm welcomes visitors; you can take a self-guided tour and even come for lunch. A store sells its produce (in season), jams and preserves, furniture, apparel and crafted goods.

We've attended two remarkable events here, not connected with the therapeutic community.

One was the Islands Folk Festival, a delightfully low-key annual summer event at the farm. With performances on 5 or 6 stages over 2 days, it's a human-scaled music festivals. Many bike in and camp in a nearby field.

We attended the 2009 Feast of Fields, an annual showcase of food and drink grown and made locally and served up as a prix fixe spread of appetizers and drinks by the dozens of south island restaurateurs and vintners. We were driven from Victoria and back in chartered buses.

The visual centrepiece of the historic 162-hectare farm is steepled green and white Providence House (built in 1921). Spacious lawns in front are the setting for large gatherings. There is a charming sitting garden in back, allotment gardens — one of many links Providence Farm has created with the larger community — numerous outbuildings with workshops and meeting rooms, stables for horses, fields, country roads and forests laced with trails.

Since opening in 1979, Providence Farm has evolved an extensive vocational training program. Some are here on a more casual basis for emotional healing. There's a culture — and a program — of horticultural therapy: "people caring for the soil, and the soil nurturing the people." The environment itself is a mode of healing. Every week some 60 volunteers come to the farm to assist.

Its many functions multiply over the farm's nearly 150-year history. For 100 years it was St Ann's School, operated by Sisters of Saint Ann, a teaching order of Catholic nuns.

TAKE5 FIVE BEST RESTAURANTS
ON VANCOUVER ISLAND
(OUTSIDE VICTORIA)

According to *Vancouver* magazine's Urban Diner 2009 awards and *EAT* magazine's 1st Annual Exceptional Eats! Awards. Vancouver's judges agreed with *EAT*'s readers' poll on the first four. Excerpted suggestions are *Vancouver*'s.

1. **Sooke Harbour House** *1528 Whiffen Spit Rd., Sooke* (250) 642-3421
"... pan-seared salmon with rosemary crème fraîche and chive oil ... sautéed morel mushrooms ... potato, beet top, and kale ... yellow-split-pea-crusted ling cod with a carrot and mint emulsion ... herb potato cake ... rhubarb strudel with daylily anglaise ... maple walnut ice cream ..."

2. **The Pointe at Wickaninnish Inn** *Chesterman Beach, Tofino* (250) 725-3100
"... Polderside Farms duck breast with potato gnocchi, blue cheese, local berries, and port ... braised Pacific rockfish with local mussels, tomato ragout, gin, basil, and saffron aioli ..."

3. **Amusé Bistro** *1753 Shawnigan Mill Bay Rd., Shawnigan Lake* (250) 743-3667
"... house charcuterie offers ... duck prosciutto and veal sausage ... local lamb [with] a mint-infused sauce paloise and an espresso-steeped demi ... ling cod with pancetta ... lemon trio of cake, curd, and sorbet ..."

4. **Long Beach Lodge Dining Room** *1441 Pacific Rim Hwy, Tofino* (250) 725-2442
"... pan-seared wild salmon atop quinoa and King prawn risotto with a watercress sauce, orange pearls, and braised baby leeks ... Dungeness crab with sea asparagus, orzo, and golden beets ..."

5. **Sobo** *311 Neill St., Tofino* (250) 725-2341
"... Killer Fish Tacos, for which Sobo has received national acclaim ... oysters encrusted with hemp seed ... frozen fish chowder for takeout ..."

The Sisters bought the property in 1864, and until 1876 St Ann's was a residential school for First Nations girls. The students apparently shunned it. The school population increased when girls attending St Ann's Academy in Victoria were orphaned and the Sisters started sending them to Cowichan.

The institution was the setting for a notable cultural exchange: First Nations girls learned to knit there. Sister Marie-Angèle is said to have been the agent of technology transfer, which the women adapted to an ancient Salish knowledge of textiles. They started making handsome waterproof wool sweaters — the basis of the flourishing Cowichan sweater industry and its many imitators. The Sister, born Marie Gauthier, learned knitting in her native Quebec.

In 1904, the farm became St Ann's Boy's School, with 30-50 boarding students. When the central block was built, the school started taking day-students. By 1950 It evolved into a co-ed day school. The school closed forever in June 1964.

Providence Farm's vision of environment, community and healing is its own, and as of 2009 the society that has operated it for 30 years became the landowner.

I've sat in the garden on a warm summer evening, looking across the fields at Mt Tzouhalem. The farm's very wholesomeness is therapeutic.

"Damn braces, bless relaxes." William Blake wrote that. Would the Sisters not agree?

Details: *Providence Farm, 1843 Tzouhalem Rd, North Cowichan. Hours, directions, contacts: http://www.providence.bc.ca/. Visitors are requested to check in at the main office in Providence House, and to call ahead for lunch.*
Islands Folk Festival: http://www.folkfest.bc.ca/.
Feast of Fields: http://www.feastoffields.com.

32   Butter Church

The abandoned stone church on Comiaken Hill near Cowichan Bay has always been called the Butter Church. A popular subject for photography, the handsome building looks like a symbol of something — but what?

The church was built in 1870 near the ancient village of *Qwumi'iqun'* (Comiaken, pronounced *cu MEE u kun*). It was a testament to the community's hard work and to the vision of pioneer missionary Peter Rondeault.

Fresh out of a Quebec Catholic seminary, Father Rondeault arrived in Cowichan Bay in 1858, by canoe, alone. His way of winning the hearts and minds of First Nations people was to throw himself headlong into the life of the community.

He was a skilled carpenter. He grew and milled wheat — he even grew tobacco. By 1870, legend has it, sales of butter from the dairy farm were enough to pay a mason and First Nations construction workers to build the church — the church that butter built. Its real name was St Ann's.

Within ten years the Catholic diocese in Victoria purchased land on Tzouhalem Rd and built another St Ann's Church. Why? One story is that Rondeault's congregation grew so rapidly the stone church became too small.

The Butter Church was on what became an Indian Reserve, and that may be part of the story. It was a special category of federal property that could not be bought or sold — which didn't sit well with the diocese.

Either way, the Butter Church was de-consecrated in 1880. Its windows and doors went to a church on Salt Spring Island, and it has mostly stood empty ever since.

A darker story about relations between First Nations and Europeans has the abandoned church for a setting.

A crowd gathered on the grassy slopes of Comiaken Hill on May 27, 1913. The Royal Commission on Indian Affairs staged an open-air hearing in front of the church.

The joint federal-provincial undertaking was to identify BC Indian Reserves that were bigger than the requirements of the population. Unoccupied lands in Indian Reserves would revert to the Crown provincial. BC wanted, in other words, to take away some of what little land had been allotted to First Nations.

A remarkable photograph in *Those Who Fell From the Sky* shows "a picture bearer retained by Chief Tsulpi'multw (Khenipsen) holding a picture of King Edward VII who he had visited in 1906."

Chief Tsulpi'multw had been one of three BC Indian Chiefs who made a 10,000 km journey to London, England where, on August 13, 1906 they were granted an audience with King Edward VII. It was a rare opportunity to make a case for redress of the land policies.

"They took the very best of our land," their petition asserted, "and gave us rock and gravel."

"I went to the King a few years ago," Chief *Tsulpi'multw's* said to the commission, "to try and get some settlement from the King, and when I got there, the King gave me this photograph. His Majesty promised to do something for us, and said he would send somebody out to look into the matter."

Other chief joined in the representation. Chief *Suhilton* (Seehaillton) said, "I myself only occupy 3½ acres, and yet the white man says I have got too much." Charley Kutsowat told the commission that "whenever he goes to get his food he gets into trouble the same as the rest, and when his cattle get out on the road they are placed in the pound, and afterwards sold."

To this day nobody has looked into those grievances. That silence, that indifference — maybe that's what the emptiness of the Butter Church represents.

Details: *The Butter Church and adjoining cemetery are maintained for visitors. W on Lemo Rd off Tzouhalem Rd.*
St. Ann's First Nations Parish, 1775 Tzouhalem Rd, has a large graveyard; Father Rondeault is buried under the chapel behind the church.

Reading: *The Cowichan Tribes' historical narrative of their search for justice is in a commissioned work,* Those Who Fell from the Sky *by Daniel P. Marshall (1999).*

Cowichan Bay 33

Cowichan Bay village occupies half of one street — the other side is an embankment — where shops and eateries, some with old-time wooden façades, back onto a cluster of docks on gloriously scenic Cowichan Bay.

A port for the Cowichan Valley beginning in the 1860s, Cowichan Bay evolved into an industrial service centre and a world-renowned salmon sport-fishing base.

A sturdy 82-metre-long former oil company jetty houses the Cowichan Bay Maritime Centre. It's the showpiece of the Cowichan Wooden Boat Society, dedicated to the restoration of old wooden boats and the construction of new ones. The centre's purpose-built *pods* have displays of the bay's marine history. Visitors are welcome to stroll around.

Several shops along the bay have a culinary theme. Cowichan Bay is a *slow-food centre* — the first community in North America so designated (in 2009) by Cittaslow, an Italian organization that promotes the use of local produce, organically grown where possible.

Two local artisans of food stand out.

True Grain Bread uses organic grains mostly grown on the island — some their own — milled on the premises and risen with organic starter yeasts. True Grain's wheat of choice is un-hybridized Red Fife. Other organic breads are made with spelt and kamut, an ancestor of durum wheat. The bakery display alone is worth a trip. The website is pleasantly informative.

Hilary's Cheese uses local organic cow and goat milk to craft an impressive assortment of cheeses — fresh-made cream cheese, white camembert-style, several tangy blues and a rinded cheese washed with local dessert cordials.

Just west of a picturesque row of waterfront cottages is a little park overlooking the industrial port and the Cowichan River estuary. There are tables and benches. Weather permitting, it's a great place for a picnic.

Details: *True Grain Bread & Mill, (250) 746-7664: http://www.truegrain.ca/. Closed Mondays.*
Hilary's Cheese and Deli, (250) 748-5992: http://www.HilarysCheese.com/.
CittaSlow: http://www.cittaslow.net/.
Cowichan Bay Maritime Centre: http://www.classicboats.org/.

34 Qu'wutsun' Cultural Centre

In this splendid cultural showpiece beside the Cowichan River, the Cowichan Tribes put their best foot forward. Behind the palisades is a constructed village that hums with activity every summer.

In a pleasant open space, contemporary carved and painted totem poles are displayed. The Salish approach to monumental carving is distinctly different from the traditions of other island cultures, and the centre has carving sheds where you can meet the artists and observe them at work.

The state-of-the-art multi-media overview Great Deeds knocked my socks off.

Ditto the story-telling guided tour by a member of the nation. Friendly and hospitable, eloquent to a degree, the hosts make it very easy for a visitor to get into the traditional mind. The presentation has a polish that suggests the tribe has its feet firmly planted in the world of today.

Culture meets commerce in the centre's offering of food. Mid-day there is a barbecue salmon lunch, served outdoors as weather permits. There's also the delightfully situated Riverwalk Café.

One of Duncan's most attractive features is the greenswathed river running through. For that we can thank the indigenous people — most of the Lower Cowichan on both sides is reserve land.

The Cowichan River was the traditional domain of this Nation. They are a people of the river as much as of the ocean. Most of their villages were on the river, and they operated as many as 21 fishing weirs.

On the outside, the Qu'wutsun' Cultural Centre doesn't make a big statement. Few signs or billboards announce its presence. Most of its visitors are with tours from other countries. The location — handy to the Island Highway and downtown Duncan — couldn't be more central.

The store is one of the best places in the valley to buy a genuine Cowichan sweater.

It's not to be missed.

Details: *Quw'utsun' Cultural and Conference Centre, 200 Cowichan Way, Duncan, (250) 746- 8119/1-877-746-8119 toll free; http://www.quwutsun.ca/. Call to reserve for the mid-day salmon BBQ. The Riverwalk Café is accessible separately.*

Fairburn Farm 35

Fairburn Farm offers comfortable lodgings in an 1880s farmhouse near Duncan on a working organic dairy farm, where a herd of water buffalo delivers the butterfat. The ample front porch looks to the west, across a garden of produce and flowers to fields that slope down to a forested creek. Mountains loom beyond. On the higher back side stand photogenic old farm buildings, relics of the original spread of nearly 500 hectares. (It's a tenth that size now.)

The Archer family has owned Fairburn Farm since 1954, and the third generation is involved in its operation as a farm destination. We stayed a weekend in the 80s. An elk's head glared at us in the front hall, a relic of Fairburn's years as a hunting lodge. In the dining room, the lamb was as local as can be — the Archers grew it right there.

We returned with our young daughter a few years later. There was a gang of kids, including the family's, and they made our Molly one of them. They raced about or cuddled the lambs. Our daughter's eyes shone with excitement.

More recently, Fairburn Farm became a locavore shrine. Its resident chef, Mara Jernigan, is a one-person cultural revolution. Mara came to Fairburn Farm in 2005, took over the guest operation and upgraded the kitchen and lodgings.

Now that Mara has moved on, Fairburn Farm will continue to provide the experience of a farm in a bed-and-breakfast setting.

Details: *Fairburn Farm, 3310 Jackson Rd, Duncan http://www.fairburnfarm.bc.ca/. Mara's blog: http://farmchefblog.com/.*

---

36   Garry Oak Preserves

The enchanting sight of spring and summer wildflowers in a woodland of mature Garry oaks is a vision not soon forgotten. Garry oak meadows are a signature landscape of the islands, and several places in the Cowichan Valley have been set aside to protect them.

Garry oaks grow from the northern Strait of Georgia in BC as far south as California, where the acorn-bearing angiosperm is known as Oregon white oak. It flourishes on drier lowlands of southeast Vancouver Island and the southern Gulf Islands.

A Garry oak tree can put down roots in rocky outcrops or deep soil. Its gnarly branches will spread in stoic isolation or form a canopy in a grove. In many places Garry oak grows with Douglas fir and arbutus.

Intact Garry oak ecosystems are, unfortunately, very rare. Their range often coincides with prime human habitat.

Only 5 percent of the islands' original Garry oak ecosystems are intact, and of the deep-soil ecosystem, less than 1.5 percent. That's according to research by the Garry Oak Ecosystems Recovery Team.

The Cowichan Valley does better than most — about 4.5 percent of the deep-soil ecosystem and nearly half the scrub oak ecosystem are intact. But of that remainder, only a tiny fraction is protected.

The Mount Tzuhalem Ecological Reserve is an 18-hectare area of rocky outcrops and scrubby oaks on the northwest side of the mountain. Syd Watts and his late partner Emily were instrumental in rescuing the site from subdivision and getting it protected in the 1980s.

The Cowichan Garry Oak Preserve is another gem, a 10.8-hectare site purchased from the Elkington pioneer farm estate by the Nature Conservancy of Canada.

A third is The Somenos Garry Oak Protected Area, just east of Somenos Marsh. The 9-hectare site, with a rare deep-soil Garry oak forest, was rescued from development by local action and purchased by BC Parks. Unlike the other two sites, it is open to public use and not to be missed, especially in spring.

Here's to the Cowichan Valley Naturalists and other groups whose volunteers turn out to pull broom and other invasive species and rebuild native plant communities. Their work is restoring these beautiful places to their original glory.

Details: *Cowichan Garry Oak Preserve: http://www.natureconservancy.ca/site/PageServer?pagename=bc_ncc_CGOP.*
Mt Tzuhalem Ecological Reserve: http://env.gov.bc.ca/bcparks/eco_reserve/mtt-zuhalem_er.html.
Somenos Garry Oak Protected Area: parking at the west end of York Rd, Duncan.
Garry Oak Ecosystems Recovery Team: http://www.goert.ca/index.php

Forest Discovery Centre   37

A working steam locomotive named Samson chuffs around a pleasant three kilometres of track by Somenos Lake. That alone is worth a stop to visit to this 40-hectare *open air museum* on the highway north of Duncan.

The museum's collection of 12 steam locies recap the industrial history of the island. Among the treasures is the Hillcrest Lumber Co. No. 1 Shay, which worked in the Cowichan Valley beginning in 1920.

The real discovery is how profoundly steam power altered the southeastern island. Steam made it possible to move the giant trees where before only animal power was available. *Railway logging* had a twin named *high-lead yarding*, where stationary *donkey engines* were used to pull the logs to trackside.

In its heyday in the 1920s, more than 1,300 km of logging railway were used at any time on the BC coast, and almost all the track was on Vancouver Island. After World War II the *hi-baller* era quickly gave way to the internal combustion engine.

The museum started as one man's hobby. Gerry Wellburn (1900-1992) was a Cowichan valley logging operator who saw the writing on the wall and amassed a huge collection of abandoned machinery. Wellburn's name is equally well-known in stamp-collecting circles. His Vancouver Island collection is one of the greats.

Details: *BC Forest Discovery Centre, 2892 Drinkwater Rd, Duncan; (250) 715-1113; bcforestmuseum.com; website has an in-depth feature on the Cowichan Valley logging camps.*
Reading: The Stamps & Postal History of Colonial Vancouver Island and British Columbia, *a coffee-table display of Gerry Wellburn's amazing collection, with his meticulously hand-lettered notations; privately published in the 80s.*

TAKE 5 LYNNE BOWEN'S FIVE
LITERARY PLACES

Author of five books of historical nonfiction, four about Vancouver Island, Lynne Bowen was co-chair of creative non-fiction writing at the University of British Columbia 1992-2006. Her next book will be a history of Italian immigration. She makes her home in Nanaimo.

1. The Dunsmuir Wellington mine was the model for the industrial setting of John Galsworthy's 1909 play *Strife*. Galsworthy's father was chair of the board of the Vancouver Coal Mining Company, which ran Nanaimo's biggest mine, the No. 1. John, a recent graduate of Oxford law school, was in a state of unrequited love when in 1891 Papa sent him to Vancouver Island to report on the labour situation following a long strike against Wellington Collieries. No doubt doors opened for Galsworthy that would be closed to anyone else.

2. The entire coal belt is the setting of my 1982 oral history *Boss Whistle: The Coal Miners of Vancouver Island Remember*. The originator had conducted nearly 120 hours of interviews, and I was asked to take over the material after I had completed my MA in history. (My thesis was about coal mining on Vancouver Island.) All the contributors are now dead. This is the book I'll be remembered for. On Alan Twigg's list of 200 significant BC works, it was #102. There never was a "boss" whistle, by the way. My husband Dick and I made up the phrase to convey a sense of the mining life. Now, when there's talk of restoring the mine, they always include it!

38 Youbou

Cowichan Lake occupies a narrow valley in the heart of the south island. Hemmed with steep slopes, the 31-kilometre-long lake has a haunting beauty. It's the picture of serenity until summer, when the lakeshore comes alive with campers and cottagers and boaters of every stripe.

Dusty through-roads carry outdoor adventurers to the west coast — on logging roads to Nitinat Lake, Carmanah-Walbran Park and Bamfield. There's a newly-paved road to Port Renfrew via the South Shore road.

3. Nanaimo society was skewered in Jack Hodgins' 1987 satiric novel *The Honorary Patron*. Jack was a Nanaimo high school teacher who had won two Governor General's awards for his comic fiction about Vancouver Island. He doesn't like to admit it, but he was the said figurehead in a local Shakespeare company, a project put together in 1984 as a tourist attraction. Shakesepare Plus contracted the black cop from Barney Miller to play Mercutio in *Romeo and Juliet*. Leon Pownell was artistic director. The festival ended up $250,000 in debt. Hodgins mined it for colourful characters.

4. In Marilyn Bowering's 1989 novel *To All Appearances a Lady*, there is a memorable reconstruction of life among the D'Arcy Island lepers, unfortunate souls whose disease was so feared they were condemned to permanent isolation. The sequence begins when a woman is left stranded on the island and seeks their help.

5. Brian Brett's charming 2009 life-in-a-day memoir *Trauma Farm: a Rebel History of Rural Life* is a brilliant anatomy of the endangered small farm tradition as well as a kaleidoscope of his and his loved ones' 18 years on a Salt Spring Island farm.

The town of Lake Cowichan, at the head of the winding Cowichan River, is the service centre for highway and lake.

Traditionally, Cowichan Lake was a resource base of both Cowichan and Ditidiaht First Nations. Then it was the haunt of rich hunters and fishers, followed by the era of the logger that began in 1912 when the E&N Railway spur reached Lake Cowichan.

Youbou (local pronunciation is *You bo*), 10 km west, memorializes the Messrs Yount (general manager) and Bouten (president), Empire Lumber Company, operators of the first sawmill there, beginning in 1914.

In 1925, the CNR line opened from Victoria to Youbou, sparking construction of a state-of-the-art sawmill. Waste wood was burned to cogenerate some of the town's power.

Youbou acquired by degrees a bank, a police station and jail, a doctor's office, a theatre, a community hall, a school — and it was one of several villages sustained by sawmills. Honeymoon Bay and Mesachie Lake were others, and Paldi was nearby.

In its heyday, the valley supported 5,000 logging and milling jobs. The whine of the cables and chuff of the steam donkeys resounded from end to end.

In short order the high-lead railway logging system cleaned out the entire valley, from lakeshore to height of land, from one end to the other. For decades Cowichan Lake was known for moonscapes of stunning proportions. It was a monument to unsustainable forestry.

The Great Depression killed the boom. After World War II, truck logging took the industry into public forestlands on the west coast. In the 50s, Camp 6 was home for a thousand loggers and family members on the south shore.

One by one the camps closed. The mills closed too, leaving Honeymoon Bay and Mesachie Lake all but deserted.

The Youbou mill closed in 2001, after more than 70 years sawing dimension and specialty lumber.

Some of the 230 workers who lost their jobs put up a fight. They formed the Youbou TimberLess Society to protest the accelerated extraction of old-growth forests and their export as raw logs. They counted the logging trucks leaving the valley loaded with wood — 450 in four days.

Youbou is a quiet community of 1,200, with cottages crowding the nearby north shore. It could get a lot busier. The Youbou sawmill site and 4.3 km of waterfront totaling 248 hectares was bought by Duncan-based Youbou Land Development Group in 2006. A 1,950-unit residential development with a commercial core got the go-ahead in June 2010. If the $1-billion project gets off the ground, Youbou will have 6,000 residents.

Youbou has three small parks that provide public access to the waterfront: Mile 77 Park, where the old CNR section manager's house stands; Price Park (5.46 hectare) on a quiet bit of shore; and Arbutus Park, with a beach and pool and lifeguards in summer. Views up the valley are magnificent.

Details: *Youbou is west of Lake Cowichan. The following distances are measured from the Youbou Rd exit on Highway 18.*
Mile 77 Park, on Creekside Dr, 7.6 km: http://www.cvrd.bc.ca/index.aspx?NID=245.
Price Park, at end of Miracle Way, intersection at 9.5 km: http://www.cvrd.bc.ca/index.aspx?NID=246.
Arbutus Park, end of Alder Cresc, intersection at 14.5 km: http://www.cvrd.bc.ca/index.aspx?NID=149.
Mosaic of Forestry Memories: http://www.forestry.mosaicprojects.net/.
Youbou TimberLess Society: http://savebcjobs.com/about.htm.

Salt Spring Island Protected Areas 39

Paula and I set out to circumnavigate Salt Spring Island by kayak and rowboat. We put in at Deep Cove, North Saanich, crossed choppy boat-infested Satellite Channel, and decided to take the route less travelled up Sansum Narrows. We assumed there were campsites along the way. Salt Spring has so many protected areas, we reasoned.

We landed on a little beach for refreshment, but within moments a power boat launched from a float across the bay. A polite but firm security chap told us what we already knew — to move on. A syndicate owns all the Salt Spring foreshore below Mt Tuam for several kilometres. We told him we were actually sitting on public land, the intertidal, but it didn't seem to register.

Geologically, Salt Spring Island is three blocks of upland, separated by fault lines. On the west side ancient rock rises to vertiginous heights, broken dramatically by Sansum Narrows. The passage was indeed narrow and rock-walled. A lively current carried us along, but it suddenly reversed, and we had to paddle like hell to make headway.

Burgoyne Bay is an opening in the narrows. The head of the bay was overhung with mountains on both sides. On the north side is Mt Maxwell, or as it is properly called, Baynes Peak.

We crossed the bay and looked for a campsite along the rocky north shore. The land sweeps up and up to the sheer rock face of Mt Maxwell. We searched for a flat spot with a haul-out nearby and found a sun-drenched grassy bluff. There were no signs posted to warn us away. We saw few people that evening, none the next morning.

What we later discovered is that there are no designated campsites anywhere on that side of the island, even though the upland around Burgoyne Bay has been the focus of intensive protection efforts. Provincial parks now protect about 750 hectares of the bay and Mt Maxwell Ecological Reserve nearly 400 ha of exquisite Garry oak woodland.

Day-use is welcome in the provincial parks, but you need permission from BC Parks to visit the ecological reserve. No wonder there were no other paddlers. Our campsite happened to be on a patch of private property. We trespassed unwittingly.

Next day we proceeded to Wallace Island, off Salt Spring's north point. A pencil of furrowed, whalebacked sandstone, Wallace has a provincial campground with a few nice sites near the little bay and a lot of gloomy ones behind.

We spent a day exploring the area and the following morning picked up a skookum current going south along Salt Spring's well-populated east side. We crossed from Nose Point to Prevost Island, hoping to cross back to Salt Spring's most popular campground, Ruckle Park. We never made it, and that was okay with us.

A tiny islet, barely 100 m by 250 m, hove into view, with a little meadow above an exquisite shell beach. A platform of wooden slats invited us to have a rest. No nails marred the smooth surface. We unfurled our ThermaRests and listened to the murmur of the wind in the firs. We looked for property signs — there were none.

We completed our circuit the next day. It's about 80 km around the island. We sinned big and had a ball.

I asked Bristol Foster, a noted conservationist and Salt Springer, about the little gem. He said it's known as Owl Islet and was once a popular rendezvous — dancing naked in the moonlight, that sort of thing. It was on the list for purchase to become part of the Gulf Islands National Park, but the owner wouldn't sell.

The following year (2008) we were in the vicinity and paddled past Owl Islet. A dock had been installed, a house was going up in the meadow, and No Trespassing signs were posted.

For future reference, there are four campgrounds around Salt Spring Island, all on the east side: Ruckle, Portland Id, Prevost Id and Wallace Id.

Details: *Maps, information about Mt Maxwell, Burgoyne Bay and Ruckle provincial parks and Wallace Id Marine Provincial Park: www.env.gov.bc.ca/bcparks, under Find a Park.*
About Mt Maxwell Ecological Reserve: on the same site, under Conservation, choose link to alphabetic listing of ecological reserves.
Mt Maxwell, Burgoyne Bay and Ruckle parks are all accessible by road. Mt Maxwell has one of the best viewpoints in the Gulf Islands, overlooking Burgoyne Bay and valley.
Portland Island and Prevost Island protected areas in the Gulf Islands National Park Reserve: http://www.pc.gc.ca/eng/pn-np/bc/gulf/index.aspx.

40 Edible Salt Spring

Salt Spring Island is no longer a place where sheep graze on the golf course. Fame has changed it and, no question, the island has lost some of its rural charm. Much remains unchanged — it's still an agricultural enclave, protected by water but accessible from Victoria in little more than an hour.

Our family visited Salt Spring Island on occasional weekends in the 1950s. We would catch the ferry *Cy Peck* from the tiny slip at Swartz Bay.

The shingled lodge at Acland's Guest House was surrounded by more than 100 acres of waterfront on Booth Bay. Across the water were the mountains of Vancouver Island.

For a child it was paradise — water warm enough to swim in summer, log rafts and a rowboat, meadows and forest to play in.

The best place to swim was near the boathouse in the Canal. The long relatively narrow tidal reach is called that, I guess, because of its shape. It isn't a proper canal that Goes Somewhere. The Canal is so shallow it empties at low tide, leaving small boats sitting on the mud.

The boathouse stood on a little spit at the mouth of the Canal. Just inside the spit, the water was deep enough that you could jump off the heaped shell beach into the swirling sand-warm current of an incoming tide.

That spit was full of clams. Early one morning I opened the door of the boathouse to discover a lot of people asleep on the floor — First Nations people, clammers from Vancouver Island.

The rocky beach teemed with life. There were crabs under every rock. Occasionally at low tide we came upon a pool made by arranging rocks in a crescent. In the pool would be a trapped dogfish or sculpin. This, I since learned, was probably a First Nations sea-ranching device.

Presiding over this magic kingdom were Marge and Bevil Acland. Of English descent, they were gracious and kindly. Marge turned out amazing meals on the wood stove. Her cooking was just the best. (Sorry, mum.)

The village of Ganges had a general store where you went up to a wide counter and ordered your supplies. A clerk would climb up a ladder with runners on the floor and ceiling.

Food continues to be a huge attraction on Salt Spring. There are many working farms. For insight into the farming life, check out poet Brian Brett's award-winning *Trauma Farm: A Rebel History of Rural Life* (D&M, 2009).

The seasonal Saturday market in Ganges showcases local produce and other edibles as well as the island's many artists.

Salt Spring is famous for its apples, and every Fall there's a one-day festival showcasing more than 350 varieties grown organically here.

Several outstanding farms are open to visits and lodging. The remarkable Salt Spring Seeds does most of its business by mail-order, but Dan Jason is happy to show visitors the organic farm, part of The Salt Spring Centre of Yoga.

Michael Ableman, a celebrated author of books about organic farming, operates Foxglove Farm on the slopes of Mt Maxwell. It's both a working organic farm, a retreat and a Centre for Arts, Ecology and Agriculture.

I have a hunch Marge and Bevil would feel right at home on today's Salt Spring.

Details: *Salt Spring Island Saturday Market: www.saltspringmarket.com.*
Salt Spring Island Organic Apple Festival: www.saltspringmarket.com/apples/.
The farm tour is fascinating.
Salt Spring Seeds: www.saltspringseeds.com
Salt Spring Centre of Yoga, 355 Blackburn Rd: www.saltspringcentre.com
Foxglove Farm, 1200 Mt Maxwell Rd: www.foxglovefarmbc.ca
Booth Bay: public access via steps at the foot of Baker Rd, W of Lower Ganges Rd, 3 km N of the centre of Ganges. Booth Canal is to the L. (In Canada all foreshore below mean high tide is public.) The boathouse is long gone; the spit much changed.

Active Pass, Salish Sea | 41

Active Pass is the S-shaped channel on BC Ferries' most-used route, between Swartz Bay and Tsawwassen. The looming rocky shores of two Gulf Islands always draw passengers onto the decks. The channel is alive, especially near the elbows at either end. The waters of Active Pass teem with waterfowl in season, and they rise in the thousands as the ferry passes, only to settle back like sheets on the swirling chuck.

A good time to be on deck is at the Georgia Strait end of Active Pass, where there are exquisite views along the outer coasts of Galiano and Mayne islands. This is where I've most often seen orcas in the Gulf Islands. Once I saw a large pod there, leaping and cavorting. The ferry stopped for a good ten minutes.

Ancient archaeological sites on Active Pass remind me that we travel on the Salish Sea. The traditional territories of Coast Salish First Nations were defined as much by the waters they used as by the lands. The inland ocean was highway, food locker and garden, field of war and slave-capture.

The domain of Salish speaking peoples is largely defined by the protected waterways between Vancouver Island and the mainland — both sides of Georgia Strait, Haro Strait, Puget Sound and eastern Juan de Fuca Strait.

The term is of recent coinage. US marine biology prof Bart Webber proposed the name in 1990 to raise consciousness about cross-border water-quality issues. The name has been adopted in both the USA and Canada. It doesn't replace the familiar names but gets folks thinking.

At a celebration in Victoria in 2010, Webber told a newspaper reporter: "A name allows you to develop a sense of place, and a knowledge of that. There are about nine million people who live on the Salish Sea, and it's crucial that we have that sense of place."

Details: *BC Ferries: http://www.bcferries.com/.*
Guidebook: *What's That Island? A Ferry Travel Guide by Bruce Whittington (Stray Feathers Press, 2010; strayfeathers.ca).*

42 Gulf Islands Geology

The Gulf Islands bathe in the inland waters of the Strait of Georgia, little worlds unto themselves.

(The 15 greater and more than 200 lesser islands between Vancouver Island and mainland BC are called that because the ambient waters were named the *Gulphe of Georgia* in 1792 by Captain George Vancouver.)

The southern Gulf Islands, the main cluster south of Nanaimo Harbour, are all aligned on the same northwest-southeast axis. The best way to see the lie of the land is to fly over it on a clear day. Regular float plane service between Vancouver and Victoria provides that opportunity. The views are simply superb.

The whole landscape looks like giant claws raked across partly-submerged clay. You'll note parallel lines of sandstone now under and now above the water. In a little bay of shale, lines of exposed strata run into a saddle of forest and then continue into a bay on the other side. Narrow valleys cradle farms that are edged by cliffy upland.

Geologists have pieced together the forces that created the distinctive alignment.

About 100 million years ago, Wrangellia Terrane snuggled into place against the North American main. The core of central Salt Spring Island is of Wrangellian origin — metamorphosed rock, igneous granites and sedimentary argillites. The rocks themselves are estimated to be about 350 million years old.

A basin formed between Wrangellia and the continental plate. It filled up with sand and other sediments. Over a period known as the Upper Cretaceous (86-65 million years ago), the deposited sediments turned into the rocks known as the Nanaimo Group — shale, sandstone and conglomerate.

Most of the southern Gulf Islands and the eastern margins of Vancouver Island are of the Nanaimo Group. The formation contained the coal belt that figures so hugely in the island's history.

Over the aeons more terranes moved into place. The result was much crunching and compacting and the uplifting of both Wrangellia and Nanaimo Group rocks. Some layers of sedimentary rock folded into either arches or basins, forming the Gulf Islands' distinctive alternation of valleys and ridges.

About 15,000 years ago the whole area was overlain by glacial ice. As the ice retreated to the northwest, it scoured valleys, exposed the layered strata of shales and sculpted the softer sandstones.

To his day the action of the sea continues to erode sandstone into fantastic formations.

Details: *Float plane service between Victoria and Vancouver centres: Harbour Air: http://www.harbour-air.com/. Westcoast Air: http://www.westcoastair.com/. Southern Gulf Islands Atlas: http://www.shim.bc.ca/gulfislands/.*

Reading: Islands in the Salish Sea: A Community Atlas, *edited by Sheila Harrington and Judi Stevenson (Victoria: TouchWood Editions, 2005).*

Foodie Bike Circuit   43

The islands' agricultural heart is a belt of sunny lowland straddling the Cowichan Valley, the Gulf Islands and the Saanich Peninsula. These largely rural areas can be linked by short ferry routes and back roads into a circuit that takes you to the centres of local cuisine and a flourishing wine industry. In *WestWorld* magazine's 2010 round-up *Top 10 B.C. Foodie Treks*, six of ten destinations were along this route.

The circuit of about 100 kilometres is at least a three-day excursion, best explored by bike toward the end of summer. Bikers face several long steep hills and unavoidable bits of highway travel. Whether you bike or drive, the rewards are many and marvellous. Amid this region's bucolic beauty are many distinctive lodgings, organic dining rooms and open farms. Beckoning you to explore along the way are beaches and parks and heights of land with sweeping views. The ferry rides are experiences in themselves.

We begin at the Swartz Bay ferry terminal — or find long-term parking at any of the six terminals on this route — and walk our bikes aboard the ferry to Fulford Harbour, Salt Spring Island.

Fulford Harbour to Vesuvius Bay: a scenic, hilly route between Fulford Harbour and Ganges follows Beaver Point, Stewart, Cusheon Lake, Beddis and Fulford-Ganges roads. Then take Upper Ganges and Vesuvius Bay roads — traffic arteries, unfortunately.

Next, take the Vesuivius-Crofton ferry.

Crofton is a quiet gem of a community in North Cowichan. The town was built (1902) on a hillside to house workers in a copper mine and smelter. Falling copper prices prompted its closure within six years, and the town languished until 1957, when it became a bedroom community for workers at the nearby pulp mill. A heritage schoolhouse has been moved there and converted to a museum. A boardwalk along the shore provides views across the water.

Crofton to Mill Bay: via Osborne Bay, Herd, Maple Bay, Tzouhalem, Cowichan Bay, Telegraph, Kilmalu rds, Highway 1 — a short stretch across the bridge near heavy traffic — Deloume and Mill Bay rds.

Ferry: Brentwood Bay-Mill Bay.

Brentwood Bay to Swartz Bay: the east side route picks up the Lochside Trail to avoid much traffic.

East side route via Peden Ln, Stellys X Rd, Wallace Dr, Amity Dr to the Lochside Trail, through Sidney and return to the Swartz Bay parking lot.

West side route via Tsartlip Dr, W Saanich Rd, Birch Rd, Chalet Dr, Lands End Rd to Swartz Bay.

Details: Victoria/Gulf Islands Cycling & Walking Map, *4th edition, Davenport Maps, Victoria; http://www.davenportmaps.com/."*
Guidebook: An Edible Journey: Exploring the Islands' Fine Foods, Farms and Vineyards *by Elizabeth Levinson (Heritage House, 3rd ed. 2009).*

Tourism BC travel planner, including accommodations. http://www.hellobc.com/ en-CA/default.htm. (Or write for the BC Accommodations Guide.)

Cowichan bike routes: http://www.naturecowichan.net/bicycle/index.html.

Top 10 B.C. Foodie Treks: http://www.mywestworld.com/living/top-10-bc-foodie-treks/.

---

44 Chemainus River Estuary

The Crofton pulp mill is an unlikely neighbourhood for the ecological jewel that is the Chemainus River estuary. It's accessible to the public just a short side trip from Highway 1.

Estuaries form at the mouths of some rivers and are among the most productive of all ecosystems — places of abundant vegetation where fish, birds and animals congregate. Despite its industrial neighbour, the Chemainus estuary is relatively untouched. Its value is enhanced by its central location within a mosaic of wetlands along the island's east coast — important habitat for migrating waterfowl along the Pacific Flyway.

Ducks Unlimited Canada ranked 442 BC estuaries according to their productivity and value. Excluding the Fraser River (the mother of all estuaries), the study put four Vancouver Island estuaries in the top 10. The Chemainus River topped the list, followed closely by the Courtenay, Cowichan and Nanaimo.

In 2009, Ducks Unlimited spearheaded the purchase of 210 hectares of farmland, intertidal flats and forest in the Chemainus estuary. The federal and provincial governments, land trusts, foundations and local businesses helped support the $3 million price tag.

The purchase provides for access for all, including the Halalt First Nation, who live above the estuary and tried unsuccessfully to buy the land. Hunting will be allowed.

Details: *Swallowfield Dr access to the Chemainus River Estuary: From Crofton: From Chaplin St intersection (km 0), follow Crofton Road N past the Catalyst pulp mill (1 km); bear R on Chemainus Rd (Highway 1A) (3.5 km) and take 1st R onto Swallowfield Rd (3.7 km). From Route 1: R at Mt Sicker Rd (km 0), L at Westholme/Chemainus Rd (0.6 km), bear L at Crofton Rd (2.3 km) and take 1st R onto Swallowfield (2.4). You can walk past the gate. Alternate access: MacDonald Rd is 1.5 km N of Chaplin St on the Crofton Rd, or 2 km S of the intersection of Westholme and Crofton rds. Turn N onto MacDonald, take a R fork and park off the road near the gate. The road is a haul road, and can be busy during working hours; a 10-minute walk leads to a delightful picnic area overlooking the estuary.*

Ducks Unlimited factsheet and map: http://www.ducks.ca/province/bc/pdf/bcchemainus.pdf.
Estuaries in British Columbia: http://www.env.gov.bc.ca/wld/documents/Estuaries_brchr06.pdf.

TAKE 5 GARY KAISER'S FIVE
WILDLIFE SPECTACLES

Gary W. Kaiser is a retired seabird biologist with the Canadian Wildlife Service based in Victoria. He is a co-author of *Birds of British Columbia* (4 vols, 1992-2001) and Seabirds of the Russian Far East (CWS 2000) and author of *The Inner Bird: Anatomy and Evolution* (UBC Press, 2007).

These are great places to see masses of water birds at particular times. A birder would likely choose places with greater diversity.

1. Qualicum Beach and Parksville during the northward migration of Black Brant and White-fronted Geese from the second half of March to mid-April.

2. Comox Harbour and south to Denman Island during April-May when herring spawn attracts a huge collection of sea ducks, Surf Scoters, White-winged Scoters and Long-tailed Duck (Oldsquaw).

3. Cleland Id, off Vargas Id, north of Torino, best-known for gulls and oystercatchers, it is the only place in southern BC where you can see Tufted Puffins, and there's also a big colony of Rhinoceros Auklets June-July. It's an ecological reserve, so you can't go on the island, but you can go around it.

4. Active Pass, between Galiano and Mayne ids, has a big population of Brandt's Cormorants during the winter, January-March, at the Victoria end, while at the far end, perhaps 1000 Arctic Loons will gather in Miner's Bay and toward the lighthouse. They moult their wing feathers in January-February and can't fly.

5. Courtenay farms have Trumpeter Swans sitting in the fields in winter. They were endangered in the 1970s but now it is easy to find spectacular flocks of 100-200, especially in potato fields!

Chemainus 45

Chemainus is the North Cowichan sawmill town that discovered how to turn sawdust to gold. Some 41 murals festoon the outside walls of its buildings, depicting the several threads of Chemainus's history. And the murals don't just tell the town's story — *they are the story*.

The murals have put Chemainus on the map. A reported 400,000 people visit per annum. Cruise ships stop at Chemainus for the murals.

A good place to begin a tour of this phenomenon is Waterwheel Park. There's a map and display beside an artistic reconstruction of the 1862 water wheel that powered Chemainus's first sawmill.

Near the tiny Chemainus Valley Museum is a lookout. The busy sawmill is directly below, and across Chemainus (Horseshoe) Bay and a bit of the Salish Sea are Thetis and Kuper islands. (BC Ferries has regular service.)

Some of the murals are strikingly good. Of those representing the town's commercial history, The Hong Hing Waterfront Store has an iconic simplicity, its weathered wooden façade hung with old ads for cigarettes and soft drinks.

Letters from the Front, the epic collage on the wall of the post office, evokes the rivers of correspondence between Chemainus and the battle-fields of World War I.

The town does have a long industrial pedigree, and at least a dozen murals take up the forestry theme. Western Forest Products' sawmill is the fifth on the property — the longest-occupied mill site in BC.

In the 1880s, moreover, the first railway logging operation on the island — near Chemainus — used the fresh-laid track of the Esquimalt & Nanaimo Railway to haul logs.

The third mill (1891-1923) marked the advent of American capital to the island. US timber tycoon Frederick Weyerhaeuser visited every year and sat on the cold deck studying the timber.

The fourth mill (1925-82) was once the largest sawmill in the British Empire. When it closed, the future looked dim.

It was during that period the mural project took shape. The originator of the idea, local retailer Karl Schutz, had been trying for a decade to get the District interested. *Paint it, and They Will Come.*

Schutz came to my office once in the first year of the murals. He was working so hard to spread the word. Bubbling with good humour and confidence, he motivated me to publish a piece about the murals — probably one of the first.

Karl went on to become a consultant to post-industrial communities worldwide. More than 60 towns have adopted Chemainus's use of a distinctive marketing brand to attract tourists.

Details: *Chemainus Festival of Murals Society, with profiles of 40 murals: http://www.muraltown.com/*
Map of murals with thumbnails of all 41: http://www.tourismchemainus.com/html/MapMural.html#

46 Joseph Mairs Memorial, Ladysmith

Ladysmith flourishes as a residential enclave while retaining one of the island's few working sawmills. An heritage streetscape forms the core of a revitalized commercial district.

Incorporated in 1904, the town was the creation of James Dunsmuir, and based on the model of Dunsmuir coal centres Wellington and Cumberland. When the Wellington mine approached exhaustion, he had some of the town's buildings relocated — at the tenants' own expense, of course — to Ladysmith.

Ladysmith was the epicentre of the island's most prolonged episode of civil strife — the coal miners' strike of 1912. The Great Strike started over safety issues at the Extension mine — Dunsmuir by this time had sold it to eastern railway interests — and quickly spread to Nanaimo and Cumberland. A pitched battle between strikers and scabs came to a head in Ladysmith on a hot August night in 1913.

After the disturbance, Ladysmith and other coal towns were occupied by militia and under martial law for months. To this day, every January a group of old-line social democrats march to the Ladysmith Cemetery and gather at the memorial to Joseph Mairs. An immigrant coal miner from Scotland, just 21 and living with his parents, Mairs was the only participant to die during the two-year strike.

He joined the Mine Workers Union of America in trying to sway the hard hearts of the mineowners and stop the ceaseless slaughter in the mines. (Methane explosions were the commonest of many ways to die.)

Young Mairs was arrested for taking part in the Ladysmith uprising. He copped a guilty plea, whereupon Judge Howay sentenced him to 16 months' hard labour in Oakalla Prison. There he soon died of a rupture in an untreated tubercular intestine.

The union raised the money for the fine monument by selling post-cards showing Mairs posing beside his bicycle and the prizes he had won in races.

Mairs' relations live on the island today, but it's thanks chiefly to hard stone that he is remembered. There are many on the island for whom Ladysmith's industrial strife is a badge of honour.

Folks in Ladysmith are crazy about history. Strange — how few traces of the Great Strike there are.

Details: *Joseph Mairs Memorial Committee, with a history of the Great Strike: http://josephmairs.ca/.*
Who Killed Joseph Mairs, Jr.? — a scholarly site: http://www.sfu.ca/labour/Home.htm
Ladysmith & District Historical Society, with a local history and inventory of heritage buildings: ladysmithhistoricalsociety.org.

Nanaimo Bastion   47

Built in 1853, the whitewashed octagonal tower in the middle of Nanaimo is the city's oldest standing building. It is also the oldest free-standing fort of the Hudson's Bay Company (HBC) and one of few such structures remaining anywhere. And it's the only fort in the HBC's far-flung fur-trading empire where coal was traded. Had it not been moved, the Bastion would surely be a National Heritage Site.

The Bastion has a symbolic quality that is central to the story of Nanaimo's founding.

The first chapter of this story belongs to the Suquash Mine. (See #98, The Suquash Mine Fiasco.)

Chapter 2 begins with a legendary conversation in the blacksmith's shop at HBC Fort Victoria. A Snuneymuxw First Nation chief was in having his rifle repaired. The smith threw some coal on the fire. The chief remarked there was plenty of that where he came from. The smith sent for Joseph McKay, second in command at the fort. The chief was invited to bring some klale (pronounced *CLA lay*, Chinook for *black*) stones to the fort. That was late 1849.

At length the chief returned, and forever after he was known as *Coal Tyee*. (*Tyee* is Chinook for *chief*.) Joseph McKay made a bee-line for Winthuysen Inlet — Nanaimo Harbour — and started searching. In June 1852 he found a seam nearly a metre wide. McKay did a little dance on it.

James Douglas, governor and HBC chief factor, dropped everything and paddled up the east coast. With him were surveyor Joseph Pemberton, mine-manager John Muir and his personal secretary. The shores and the harbour were "*one vast coal-field*," Douglas wrote.

By the end of August McKay, age 23, was in charge of it. Families evacuated from Fort Rupert began arriving a week later. The first shipment of coal cleared the harbour September 10.

As the failed colony at Fort Rupert was being abandoned, Colviletown sprang into life. It was named for a London HBC bigwig. The name was dropped within a few years. It was always called Nanaimo — after the Hul'qumi'num Salish name for the domain of the Snuneymuxw First Nation.

McKay was a force of nature. Houses, stores, a school, a saltery went up in short order. Nanaimo's instant success put the colony back on course to having a settlement within five years. It might have gone the other way.

Getting the Snuneymuxw First Nation to sell the coalbeds and townsite was not so simple. It took Douglas nearly two years of negotiation, and then the purchase of about 2,500 hectares "from Commercial Inlet 12 miles up the Nanaimo River" was documented with the marks of First Nations leaders on blank paper. James Douglas signed as chief factor of the company.

Construction of the Bastion started in February 1853, soon after the hangings at Gallows Point (#49). The Bastion was the local office of the

HBC, an arsenal, a refuge for miners and their families in case of attack. It didn't last long — the HBC pulled out of the coal business in 1862.

In short order Nanaimo was a city — one where people lived right on top of their livelihood. Nanaimo remained a coal-mining town for a century. The downtown is laced with tunnels. There were shaft openings and slopes all around the Bastion.

There it stands — a reminder of that heritage, one relatively unchanging thing in an ever-changing city.

Details: *The Nanaimo Bastion is usually open to visitors in season. The building had to be closed in 2010 for extensive repairs; the noon cannon continues seasonally.*

Nanaimo Museum: in the Vancouver Island Conference Centre, 100 Museum Way, (250) 753-1821; nanaimomuseum.ca; displays and local literature about King Coal; website has an interactive virtual tour of the Bastion.

List of coal mines and landmarks in the Nanaimo area, with precise co-ordinates: http://en.wikipedia.org/wiki/List_of_coal_mines_and_landmarks_in_the_Nanaimo_area.

Voices of the Snuneymuxw First Nation: http://www.snuneymuxwvoices.ca/english/index.asp.

48   Tonight at the Port Theatre

Vancouver Island's best performance hall is Nanaimo's civic theatre, The Port. It seats 800 people and is an acoustic gem. Its program leans to showcasing local and regional talents.

Will She ever return to play her home town? With her husband? I see it in bright lights: *Tonight at the Port — Diana Krall and Elvis Costello.*

I've tracked the career of Mister Diana Krall since the 1978 Armed Forces Tour with the Attractions at the UBC War Memorial Gym, Vancouver. He's done okay — 36 studio albums, a successful TV music talk show, Spectacle, put together with their close buddy Sir Elton John.

Caught Ms Krall in Victoria with a potent little quartet. She sits down with authority. The first wicked chords announced a genius talent. She half turns to sing. Utter mastery of the microphone. All sotto voce, the under-voice — less is more. And that trademark phrasing.

This master of classic jazz has gone into periods of singing her own songs in a meditative cast and has branched out into producing Barbra Streisand's latest, a set of duets with herself, and a solo album of samba vocals.

To hear Krall cover Joni Mitchell's classic A Case of You, chording Mitchell's celestial anthem, throwing away that killer line, "I drew a map of Canada/Oh, Canada" — it says something to me about succession and continuity. I hear a subtext about how hard it is to go away and not to return.

Ms Krall recently published a short travel piece on Tofino — "my favorite place" — in the *Telegraph.*

The writing is on the wall. She belongs to the world. They live in New

York and London. Not so much Vancouver Island. They will visit.

I can't wait to see it — *Live At the Port Tonight*.

Details: *Port Theatre http://www.porttheatre.com/.
Diana Krall: http://www.dianakrall.com/.
Elvis Costello: http://www.elviscostello.com/.*

Gallows Point   49

Protection Island is a hidden jewel in Nanaimo Harbour. The island, closest of the three that protect the harbour, is a residential enclave with a decidedly rustic feel. Just 1.5 kilometres across, its flat, forested terrain is crisscrossed with little lanes and pathways. For those who don't paddle to town, there's regular foot ferry service. Visitors are welcome, although there are few amenities.

On the south side of Protection is little Gallows Point Park. Beyond expanses of beach (at low tide) are great views of passing vessels and the working harbour. Directly south is the Nanaimo River estuary, bordered by the sandstone finger of Duke Point.

Gallows Point commemorates the first executions in the Colony of Vancouver Island. A public hanging there on January 17, 1853 followed the relentless pursuit and speedy trial of two First Nations men.

The story of the gallows speaks volumes about our heritage.

HBC shepherd Peter Brown was killed in November 1852 on Christmas Hill, 5 km north of Fort Victoria. A Snuneymuxw First Nation man and a man of Cowichan were said to be the perps.

Fear grew that First Nations were going to attack the tiny settlement of Fort Victoria, or the fledgling HBC farms, or Colviletown (Nanaimo) or Fort Rupert.

James Douglas took charge of a posse and, on a bitter cold January 5, his flotilla departed Esquimalt Harbour. It comprised the paddle-steamer Beaver towing the HBC brigantine *Recovery*, accompanied by three small vessels from a 36-gun warship. On board were 120 British sailors and marines and 20 Voltigeurs, French-Canadian militiamen.

The force arrived in Cowichan Bay the next day. Douglas sent messengers to the villages. The following day a war party appeared in a fierce show. But no shots were fired, and the residents were persuaded to give up the one suspect they were harbouring.

How? Disciplined intimidation. Douglas had a feel for theatre. With his force deployed behind him, he made a little speech:

Hearken, O Chiefs! I am sent by King George who is your friend, and who desires right only between his tribes and your men. If his men kill an Indian, they are punished. If your men do likewise, they must also suffer.

Give up the murderer, and let there be peace between the peoples, or I will burn your lodges and trample out your tribes. *(Emphasis added.)*

Ponder that threat for a moment. Does it seem more than a little out of proportion to the crime? After all, Brown had, it was bruited, provoked the attack by insulting a woman or women in the First Nations party.

Douglas's policy was to *avoid* using direct force against First Nations groups. He decried the bloody confrontations erupting in the northwest United States. The Brown case was a test — and a showpiece — of Hudson's Bay Company justice.

Douglas isolated the wrongdoers in an almost surgical procedure.

The party arrived in Nanaimo Harbour on the evening of January 9. The Snuneymuxw First Nation leaders were less than forthcoming, and the suspect escaped. Douglas took hostage the chief his father and "another influential Indian." The troops deployed. They advanced by land to the suspect's village. It was deserted, the abandoned houses filled with winter provisions. The inhabitants "were now completely in our power," Douglas wrote.

The chase led up a snowy creek bed to a hiding place under a log. The troops withdrew without incident. The two men were tried aboard the Beaver, Justice Douglas presiding. Officers of the force served as the jury of peers. The men were hanged the same day with the Snuneymuxw people watching.

Details: *Protection Id ferry, hourly from Nanaimo Harbour dock, Promenade Dr near Front St, opposite the mall.*
City of Nanaimo web page on Protection Island: http://www.nanaimoinformation.com/protection-island.php.
Biggs Park and Jack Point Park, at the end of the Duke Pt peninsula, have more good vantage points for views of the harbour; a bit of a trek through Nanaimo's heavy industry zone.

50 Newcastle Island

Newcastle Island is the *Stanley Park* of Nanaimo — a 336-hectare forested oasis near the downtown, laced with trails and studded with viewpoints.

One of the island's notable landmarks is a wooden pavilion. Built by the Canadian Pacific Steamship Co in the 30s, it was dance hall that invited folks to have a good time on a summer evening. You can almost hear it — laughter and music floating across the harbour, a chorus of *Happy Days Are Here Again*, lights shimmering on the water, the antique steamship *Charmer* tied up in Mark Bay, a floating hotel.

The restored pavilion is the focal point and information centre for Newcastle Island Marine Park. You can get a decent salmon burger there, as well as camping supplies.

The island's 22 kilometres of well-marked trails reveal abundant evidence of diverse economic life. There are the shell middens of two Salish winter fishing camps, evidently occupied during the herring season.

Coal mines were worked for a few years in the 1850s and 1870s.

Newcastle Island sandstone was used in the ornate façades of Romanesque architecture favoured for public buildings of the day. The 1895 Nanaimo Courthouse, designed by Francis Rattenbury, is a showpiece of Newcastle sandstone.

In the 1920s giant sandstone millstones were quarried separately for use in groundwood pulp mills.

After 1900 Japanese fishers built salteries on the island. Preserved herring (in winter) and salmon (in summer) found good markets in Asia.

Japanese residents started a shipbuilding yard that flourished until World War II.

The park has many amenities — swimming beaches and a playground; a store in the pavilion; a 15-site walk-in campground close to the ferry dock; public moorage. There are gorgeous views to the east.

In the summer, there's frequent passenger service from the Nanaimo Harbour Ferry dock in Maffeo-Sutton Park.

Out of season you'll have to to bring or rent a vessel. At low tide, you can walk from Protection Island.

Details: *Newcastle Island Marine Provincial Park: http://www.env.gov.bc.ca/ bcparks/explore/parkpgs/newcastle/.*
Nanaimo Harbour Ferry: http://www.nanaimoharbourferry.com/.
Nanaimo Courthouse: 36 Front Street.

Parksville-Qualicum Sand | 51

The scenic stretch of east coast between Parksville and Qualicum Beach is sometimes called Oceanside. If you're looking for sand, *fill your boots*. For 20 kilometres there are intermittent sandy beaches facing the Strait of Georgia. Rathtrevor Beach on Craig Bay is easily a kilometre wide at low tide.

The summertime scene in Parksville-Qualicum is tops in family waterfront destinations. It's the atmosphere, the exhilarating views — but mainly the sand. I like the way on a sunny summer day the sand warms the incoming tide — water that is otherwise chilly at any time of year.

In July the whole community focuses on sand — fashioned into works of art at the sand sculpting competition. This is the real thing, the Canadian Open of sand sculpting. The winner gets a place in the world championships.

The sand sculptures are created over a weekend using just sand and water, then on display for a month. They display remarkable detail, and some are true originals. Fantasy is a popular theme. Some memorialize events or causes. The best sculptures deliver powerful impressions. There's a poignancy about their transience — here today, gone tomorrow.

This is campground heartland. Rathtrevor Beach Park is probably the most popular of all BC Parks' campgrounds — you have to book in advance. The park comprises 347 hectares varied environments — forest, field and the spacious beach on Craig Bay. At some times of year the beach is strewn with sand dollars. It's quite a sight. There are interpretive programs for kids.

Other notable campgrounds are a bit away from the busy beach scene. Englishman River Falls is 13 km south of Parksville; Little Qualicum Falls, 20 km west on the Port Alberni Rd. Both rivers have sculpted exquisite falls and pools in bedrock; campgrounds are nearby.

Details: *The Oceanside route (Highway 19A) begins 6 km west of Nanoose Bay and extends to Campbell River.*
Rathtrevor Beach Provincial Park: http://www.env.gov.bc.ca/bcparks/explore/ parkpgs/rathtrevor/.
Quality Foods Canadian Open Sand Sculpting Competition and Exhibition: http://www.parksvillebeachfest.ca/. Parking at the Parksville Community Park. Admission by donation to the gated competition exhibition.

52 Brant Wildlife Festival

The vast shallows of the Parksville-Qualicum shoreline are an important wildlife area. Every March they attract thousands of Black Brant migrating north from their winter grounds in California and Mexico.

The Pacific herring spawn attracts clouds of geese, gulls and other seabirds, raptors and sea mammals. Brants — little sea geese — feed, rest, socialize and fly on. Humans do the same after flocking to view the spectacle during the Brant Wildlife Festival.

A month-long celebration in Qualicum Beach, the Brant Festival stages tours and excursions, talks, a photography competition, wildlife wood-carving competitions, special events for kids and other feathery, furry pursuits. The festival recently celebrated its 20th anniversary.

The initial spark came in a period of rapid growth in this well-heeled bed-room community. With 40,000 people living in Parksville-Qualicum, its most desireable spots for human habitat — near the extensive waterfront, with views of Georgia Strait — are also the most productive habitat for wildlife.

The Nature Trust of BC took the lead in assembling lands in what became the Parksville-Qualicum Beach Wildlife Management Area (WMA). The Trust has been involved in buying salmon spawning habitat on Englishman River since 1978 and in the 1980s began buying bits of the estuary totaling 77 hectares.

The Parksville-Qualicum Beach WMA knits together many small parcels assembled since the 1980s from the Little Qualicum River estuary to Madrona

Point. Its protection extends to 17 kilometres of shore, mainly intertidal areas.

Several viewing platforms along Qualicum Bay have displays with more information about the agencies and groups involved with the preservation of wildlife habitat.

And for a taste of the good life, an excursion to the 28-ha Milner Gardens is recommended. The Qualicum Beach estate of Alberta oil landlord Ray Milner and Veronica Milner includes 4 hectares of sumptuous gardens overlooking Georgia Strait and a remnant old-growth Douglas fir forest. Tea is served in the charming house.

Details: *Brant Wildlife Festival: http://www.brantfestival.bc.ca/.*
The Nature Trust of British Columbia: http://www.naturetrust.bc.ca/.
Vancouver Island's Englishman River: http://www.naturetrust.bc.ca/articles/Englishman%20River%20case%20statement%20pdf.pdf .
Milner Gardens and Woodland, 2179 West Island Highway, Qualicum Beach, (250) 752-8573; http://www.viu.ca/MilnerGardens/index.asp. Open from April 1.

Horne Lake Caves — 53

The Horne Lake Caves, about 25 kilometres west of Qualicum Beach, are the only place on the island (one of two in BC) where guided tours of caves are offered in a provincial park.

Vancouver Island has more than 1,500 known caves. The concentration of caving destinations is unique in Canada and the stuff of legend among cavers worldwide.

Three principal caves are protected in Horne Lake Caves Park, with a buffer zone totaling 158 hectares.

The Riverbend Cave is gated but accessible in summer via 90-minute guided tours by the park operators. These are billed as family tours, but not suitable for young children. The 3-hour Adventure is offered year-round, and there are Extreme tours that involve rappelling.

It's a fascinating world of swirling earthtones and marble-like surfaces, with stalactites hanging tight and mounded stalagmites.

Two smaller caves without gates are open year 'round. (Access to one of the caves has been restricted due to a blocked trail.) There you're on your own. The openings are negotiable by any reasonably fit individual. I noted that the air below was always fresh.

The most rudimentary rules include these: cave in groups of 3-6; bring at least two flashlights; wear helmets and old clothing; dress warmly; take nothing but pictures and avoid leaving traces of your visit.

Details: *Horne Lake Caves Provincial Park: The parking lot is 14 km W of Highway 19 on Horne Lake Rd; then a walk to the caves. In winter, the operator's office is at the Horne Lake Campground, 13 km W of Highway 19.*
Access map: http://www.env.gov.bc.ca/bcparks/explore/parkpgs/horne_lk/.

TAKE 5 BILL TURNER'S FIVE GEMS
OF PRESERVED PROPERTY

Bill Turner is founding executive director of The Land Conservancy of BC (TLC), a land trust that raises money to buy properties of outstanding natural, heritage and recreational value. Since the society's foundation in 1997, TLC has preserved more than 80 BC properties totalling some 35,000 hectares. (Some were bequeathed.) TLC also holds covenants for landowners who practice long-term conservation by amending title to their properties. In recognition of TLC's success in preservation, Bill Turner received the Order of Canada in 2005. By profession he is a real estate agent.

1. Gowlland Point/Brooks Point Regional Park, South Pender Island
A rocky coast of five hectares near the east end of Pender with magnificent views. It's an outstanding place to view sea mammals — orcas, sea lions, seals. The park (see www.crd.bc.ca/parks) conserves open meadow with gorgeous spring wildflower displays. TLC bought Gowlland Point and is just now negotiating the purchase of the final property between it and Brooks Point. Preservation of nature is where we spend most of our energy and resources.

2. Abkhazi Garden, Victoria
One of the world's great small gardens is in a Victoria suburb. An exquisitely beautiful place, it has a wonderful tranquility. We are so pleased TLC was able to purchase the property and that it is involved in opening the garden and house to the public. We own and operate several heritage properties on Vancouver Island.

3. Keating Farm Estate, Cowichan Valley
Of several farms TLC operates, Keating has the most agricultural and livestock ambience, nature, wildlife and history. It epitomizes all that TLC is trying to preserve — nature, agricultural heritage, built heritage and public involvement, all in one place.

Beware of inaccuracies in the text.
Cave tours: http://www.hornelake.com/caving_programs.htm. Check the opera-
tor's website for weather advisories.

4. **South Winchelsea Island**

TLC's first acquisition project was a 10-hectare island in the Strait of Georgia north of Nanaimo. South Winchelsea is basically untouched. It has a rare intact wildflower community. The island is too small to have been logged like most of the other Gulf Islands, and it's too far from Lanzville for many deer to swim over. There is a cottage on the island that we rent year-round. We provide water transport to and from. In winter, several hundred male sea lions gather on nearby rocks. In spring I've seen as many as 28 bald eagles there at one time. We have three other rental properties on Vancouver Island.

5. **Sooke Potholes**

The Potholes are a series of swimming holes carved in rock by the Sooke River. It's an outstanding recreation area. TLC has a great interest in preserving properties for recreation. We transferred the property to CRD Parks but have assumed the role of campground operator. Securing the property took some creativity. Our involvement began when a planned development failed and a lending institution foreclosed on its mortgages. TLC had the opportunity to buy the interest of the second mortgage. We had to raise $1.35 million over a week-end. It was Earth Day, and Alison Spriggs spent most of it on her cell phone lining up 11 lenders. I was in touch at every step by telephone — from England — to do the deals. Eventually TLC bought out the first mortgage.

54 Old Country Market, Coombs

Coombs is a rural community inland of Parksville, based on logging but with relic orchards planted by the Salvation Army in the early 1900s.

Its chief claim to fame is the Old Country Market, where goats graze on the grass roof.

Owner Larry Geekie is a third-generation Coombser. He tells how when they built the produce store, his father-in-law put sod on the roof to remind him of Norway.

The goats were an idea cooked up over a jug of wine in the run-up to the Coombs Fall Fair. A friend volunteered some pet goats. "I had to drive them home at the end of the day," Larry recalls.

The rest is history. People come from all around to see the goats (in season). Their phenomenal popularity was totally unforeseen. "It just happened."

Thanks to the goats, the market has grown "creatively," Geekie says, with many "organic" additions. (The building inspector recently caught up with them and put an end to that.)

There's a local smoked salmon shop, a bakery, a restaurant — and a second on the way. A specialty grocery that stocks interesting European imports. An ice cream shop, a gift shop, a garden accessory shop, a shop that sells Chinese antiques.

And of course the original grocery, which buys both imported and local veg. (It may be organic but is not certified.)

This wholesome family-run business has nothing to do with the commercial slum next door, although that, too, is all about the economic power of goats on the roof. *Graze them, and it will come.*

Details: *The Old Country Market in Coombs is 9 km W of Parksville, 7 km W of Highway 19, on the Old Alberni Road (Highway 4A).*
Hours, directions: http://www.oldcountrymarket.com/index.php.

MacMillan Provincial Park 55

Cathedral Grove is the most outstanding easily-accessible old-growth forest on the island. The imposing 15-hectare forest of giant Douglas fir, western redcedar, western hemlock and grand fir trees flanks the Port Alberni road (Highway 4) just west of Cameron Lake. Douglas firs and cedars up to 4.5 metres in diameter and estimated to be 800 years old are protected in 301-hectare MacMillan Provincial Park.

The Nanaimo-Alberni road was punched through the ancient forest in 1910, while the E&N Railway's Alberni line was being built along the north shore of Cameron Lake, complete with a railway resort, the Chalet, at the east end. Cathedral Grove was beginning to be touted as a tourist destination even then.

Despite petitions and testimonials urging its protection, it was part of the E&N Railway Lands and remained in private hands for decades. The story goes that in Port Alberni, H.R. MacMillan got into a shouting match with the relentless tourism lobby. He caved in with the immortal words, "All right, you can have the goddamn grove."

The park has become a hugely popular roadside stopping place, attracting some 300,000 visitors annually. It has so many visitors it's in danger of being loved to death. The foot traffic is compacting the soils.

That's nothing compared to the devastation wrought by flooding and high winds. "Logging of the remainder of the upstream valley has resulted in significant damage to the Cameron River's course and the adjacent forest," retired BC Parks forester Kerry Joy wrote in 2005.

"In 1990, extreme runoff from a tropical storm caused extensive flooding and high winds resulted in 6 ha of blowdown and streambank erosion. In 1996 high winds estimated at 110 km/h resulted in windfall and broken treetops, causing extensive damage to the grove and surrounding forest."

I have had a near-religious experience in the ancient forest, and not because its towering trunks resemble columns in a gothic cathedral. It's more about becoming aware of the dance of life and death. Fallen giants are an essential part of the nutrient cycle in a self-perpetuating old-growth forest. The problem in Cathedral Grove is that so many have fallen in recent years.

Here's another reason to treasure MacMillan Park. Surveying the island, it's shocking how little old-growth Douglas fir forest has been protected. This is the heartland of the Douglas Fir Empire. It was the economic foundation of thousands of jobs, dozens of communities and many a fortune beside MacMillan's.

Standing in Cathedral Grove you get a sense of the island's primal magnificence.

Details: *MacMillan Provincial Park: http://www.env.gov.bc.ca/bcparks/explore/parkpgs/macmillan/.*
A Swedish website with a radical conservationist POV: http://www.cathedral-grove.eu/text/01-Cathedral-Grove-1.htm.

56   Oysters of Fanny Bay

Fanny Bay is the epicenter of the Comox Valley's flourishing shellfish industry. The waters of Baynes Sound are shallow and relatively warm in the shelter of Denman Island — just right for growing oysters and clams.

Fanny Bay oysters are served in restaurants and oyster bars the world over. And Mac's Oysters has been growing them here since 1947, both on the beach and by aquaculture. Mac was Joe McLellan and now a fourth generation of the family is involved in the diverse operation. Mac's specialty is the Signature Beach Oyster, meaty and "deliciously salty."

Down the road at Fanny Bay Oysters, it's the Fanny Bay, a farmed oyster of "pronounced sweetness and saltiness with a refreshing finish."

Stellar Bay Shellfish markets a Kyusshi oyster, with a distinct "buttery texture, rich & salty with a sweet, mildly fruity finish."

At Pentlatch Seafoods the specialty is beach-grown Komo Gway, a "plump oyster with a dark velvety mantle, medium salt and a nice cucumber finish."

Every June the one-day Comox Valley Shellfish Festival attracts a crowd with its shucking competition and nine-chef, nine-dish shellfish extravaganza. In 2010 the chefs prepared 200 dinners, a sell-out at $120 a seat. Among the participating establishments:

• Atlas Cafe, 250 6th Street, Courtenay (250) 338-9838.
• Avenue Bistro, 2064 Comox Ave, Comox (250) 890-9200.
• Blackfin Pub at the Marina, 132 Port Augusta St, Comox (250) 339-5030.
• Locals Restaurant, 364 8th St, Courtenay (250) 338-6493.

North of Fanny Bay is Buckley Bay, where the ferry departs for Denman Island, with connections to Hornby Island. Between there and Union Bay, Highway 19A runs along the shore. The views of agricultural Denman Island are captivating. The intervening passage is often busy with the routines of aquaculture. There are places to stop and drink it in.

All this clean, green industry could be threatened by a proposed underground coal mine directly upslope from Fanny Bay. The Raven Project has drawn deep concern and sharp criticism from local residents.

One concern in Fanny Bay is about a plan to wash the mined coal prior to trucking it to Port Alberni. Washing will draw heavily on local water supplies.

Then there's the issue of the contaminants that will be generated, especially highly-toxic coal dust.

There's a fear it will have a disastrous impact on the shellfishery, with its delicate tolerances and sterling reputation for purity. The proponent has promised to address these issues. Local citizens fear the planning process will not provide the safeguards they require.

Details: *Mac's Oysters: http://www.macsoysters.com/.*
Fanny Bay Oyster Co: http://www.fannybayoysters.com/. Retail store.
Stellar Bay Shellfish: http://www.stellarbay.ca/.
Pentlatch Seafoods: http://komogway.com/.
Guide to BC oyster varieties and growers: http://www.pacifickiss.ca/about-bc-oysters/bc-oyster-buyers-guide.
Comox Valley Shellfish Festival: http://www.comoxvalleyshellfishfestival.ca.

CoalWatch Comox Valley: http://www.coalwatch.ca/.
Raven Underground Coal Project: http://www.theravenproject.ca.

Ford's Cove, Hornby Island   57

There are islands it takes two ferries to reach — Cortes, Hornby, Saturna. And that makes them different. Something sure does.

Hornby Island has a wholesome, paradisal quality — it's the kind of place people search all their lives to find. With gorgeous beaches and cliffside trails and an abundance of natural wonders, I think it is the most beautiful Gulf Island. The rocks alone are worth a visit.

The whole island is just 3,000 hectares in size. From the ferry dock at Shingle Spit to the end of the road at Ford's Cove is 13 kilometres. You have to drive around the landmass at the centre of Hornby, Mt Geoffrey with its splendid L-shaped escarpment. The island's middle is roadless, laced with hiking and biking trails.

The road winds along the shore and through cottage country, past farms and artists' studios, past a bakery where you can sit in a heavenly garden and eat fresh blackberry pie.

Past the Co-op store and the funkiest shopping mall ever. Past Tribune Bay and clothing-optional Little Tribune — reportedly the sunniest beaches in the Gulf Islands.

Past Olsen's Farm where every summer the Hornby Festival brings international talent to an outdoor stage. Past an underground house on a cliff and various hand-made free-form houses.

Finally down a long hill to Ford's Cove marina, cottages and campground. We pass a cluster of cabins and a washhouse to reach the campground, a nice clean field bordered by a forest of sizeable Douglas firs. In the night, the place is utterly dark and quiet.

A sandstone shelf extends from Ford's Cove to Heron Rocks. A spectacle unfolds of galleries and fretworks carved by the waves of millennia. "The honeycombed surfaces we see today in the De Courcy [Formation] sandstone," resident geologist Olivia Fletcher writes, "are produced by the weathering of a carbonate-filled network of cracks. The sea washes out the softer sand, leaving the sandstone, lithified with more cement, standing out in relief."

A large chiseled and painted pictograph is barely visible in morning light but stands out vividly when I return in the evening. It depicts a sea monster.

To do justice to Hornby's amazing sandstone shores requires a day in a vessel. Come to think of it, there are few islands around which I'd rather mess in a boat.

I haven't mentioned the splendid peninsular Helliwell Provincial Park with its conglomerate cliffs — or its 2,800 hectares of protected foreshore so popular with divers.

Hornby's permanent residents now number about 900 while the summer-only crowd swells the population to 4,000. Here's hoping its delightful character survives.

Details: *Ford's Cove Marina: http://www.fordscove.com/index.html.*
Tribune Bay Provincial Park : http://www.env.gov.bc.ca/bcparks/explore/parkpgs/tribune/.
Mt Geoffrey Escarpment Provincial Park: http://www.env.gov.bc.ca/bcparks/ explore/parkpgs/mt_geoffrey/.
Mt Geoffrey Nature Park (Comox Valley RD) trail map: http://www.rdcs.bc.ca/ uploadedFiles/Parks/Park_Information/MtGeoffreyTrailMap06.pdf.
Hornby Festival: http://www.hornbyfestival.bc.ca/.
Helliwell Provincial Park: http://www.env.gov.bc.ca/bcparks/explore/parkpgs/helliwell/.
Reading: Hammerstone: A Biography of Hornby Island *by Olivia Fletcher (Edmonton: NeWest Press, 2001).*
Hornby Island Bald eagle nest cam: http://www.hornbyeagles.com/.

58 The Comox Valley

The Comox Valley is a fertile strip of lowland prairie and Douglas fir forest between the Vancouver Island Mountains and the Strait of Georgia. A farming district and former logging centre, it has a salubrious climate and stupendous surroundings, with the alpine reaches of Forbidden Plateau and Mt Washington on one side and the seawashed shores of Denman and Hornby islands on the other. No wonder people have been flocking to the valley to live.

The heart of the Comox Valley is lush bottomland and estuary where the Puntledge and Tsolum rivers join and, as the 3-kilometre-long Courtenay River, empty into Comox Harbour.

The lowland and shallows comprise one of BC's most abundant wildlife areas. It's especially enriched by wintering waterfowl. The waters teem with fish and are famous for shellfish.

Waterfront parks provide excellent views of the harbour and its gorgeous surroundings.

From the Royston Viewing Stand, 6 km southeast of Courtenay city centre, Comox town centre is 3 km northeast, on the opposite shore, sheltered by long-necked Goose Spit. The harbour's navigable water is between the goose's head and the Comox pier. Texada Island is visible to the east across Georgia Strait. Beyond are the snowy peaks of the Coast Mountains.

Dyke Road Park, Comox, has viewing platforms overlooking the estuary — a sumptuous spot, with Comox Glacier dominating the western horizon.

European settlement began with 10 miners from Nanaimo in 1861. Only one endured — George Mitchell. He started a farm at the mouth of the river and married a First Nations woman. More would-be farmers were dropped into the valley in 1862 by the Royal Navy.

Explorer Robert Brown visited in August 1864 to find "monster potatoes, onions as large as Spanish ones, parsnips, wheat and oats full headed, and sound turnips, splendid butter & milk . . . During our visit hay was being cut in the meadows at the river's mouth for the Victoria market."

The district continues to attract new settlers at a brisk rate. The Comox Valley Regional District (2009 estimated population 64,084) grew 16 percent between 2001 and 2010 — and it's projected to grow as much again by 2020. While that's good news for the economy, it may not necessarily good for the environment.

Random unplanned development is having a huge impact on the valley's ecosystems. A 2007 study found that 60 percent of pristine sensitive ecosystem lands remaining in 1991 were disturbed by 2002, while 97 percent of high-value second-growth forest and seasonally-flooded agricultural fields had become fragmented.

"The continued loss of biodiversity," the Comox Valley Land Trust warned, "will eventually undermine nature's ability to provide essential environmental services."

While on Comox Road, be sure to pick up a hamburger at George's Food Bar, a Courtenay institution that is the islands' least likely place to have the best anything. It's at 540 Comox Rd — but don't look for a number, or even a sign. You will find George's *when you know what you are looking for.* From downtown Courtenay, take 5th St east over the bridge — the first right is Comox Rd. In the first building on the east side, the low white building with the blue trim, the nearest window is George's. The clerk, who is also a cook, and who may be George, sometimes comes a bit closer to the window, writes nothing down, adds nothing up, just gives you a total and arguably the best hamburger on the island — a hamburger with plenty of fried onions, lettuce, tomato, dressing and juice. Cash only.

Details: *Comox Valley Regional District website has details and maps of Royston Viewing Stand and Dyke Rd Park: http://www.comoxvalleyrd.ca/section_comserv/content.asp?id=1986&parent=80&sub_collection=91.*
Courtenay Riverway Heritage Walk guide: http://www.discovercomoxvalley.com/culture/documents/CourtenayRiverwayHeritageWalkbrochure.pdf
Reading: The Wilderness Profound: Victorian Life on the Gulf of Georgia *by Richard Somerset Mackie (Victoria: Sono Nis Press, 1995).*
Sensitive Ecosystem Inventory for the Comox Valley: http://www.cvlandtrust.org/rcs-project.htm.

The I-Hos Gallery is an attractive showplace for First Nations art, carving, jewellery, textiles and clothing on the beautifully-situated Comox Harbour land of the K'ómoks First Nation. A powerfully carved and painted figure of the double-headed sea serpent *I-Hos* is part of the façade facing Comox Rd. Made by Calvin Hunt and associates in 1995, the figure illustrates a cultural hybridity unique on the islands.

The Comox Valley marks one of the island's important cultural boundaries — between the northernmost Salish communities and the southernmost Kwakwaka'wakw. The boundary used to be much further north, around Kelsey Bay. Sometime before European settlement — it may have started before the first European visitors in the last quarter of the 18th century — the valley's natural riches prompted others to encroach. Comox Harbour became the domain of three First Nations.

The Pentlatch First Nation was a powerful Salish people whose winter village was on the lower Puntledge River. They suffered a succession of disasters. They had a ruinous back-and-forth feud with Nuu-Chah-Nulth people in the Alberni Valley. They were ravaged by European diseases. Their northern neighbours the Comox First Nation — an allied Salish people — encroached on their lands. The Comox nation had five winter villages on Johnstone Strait. They began moving south and settling in the Comox Harbour area. They fought with the Pentlatch, who at length made peace and threw in their lot with their oppressors.

The Comox were forced in turn into making alliances with an oppressor — the Lekwiltok First Nation, a Kwakwaka'wakw people previously living even further north, on the mainland coast. The Lekwiltok migrated south and were a terror everywhere their swift canoes probed. The Lekwiltok took possession of the former northern lands of the Comox and availed themselves of the bounty of Comox Harbour in season. By marriage and colonization the Lekwiltok absorbed the Comox, who lost their Salish identity. Today the K'ómoks First Nation has both Kwakwaka'wakw and Salish affiliations.

A catastrophic smallpox epidemic began in the spring of 1862. One half of the Comox people died and seven in ten Kwakwaka'wakw people, coastwide. The Pentlatch people all but disappeared. It was a time of great disorder for First Nations. As in the Cowichan Valley, the colonial government promoted settlement in the wake of the epidemic — without bothering to buy the land from its rightful owners. "It is no easy matter," visitor Robert Brown wrote in 1864, "to answer the question satisfactorily when an intelligent Indian looks up in your face and asks 'Had you no good land of your own that you come and deprive us of ours?'"

Details: *I-Hos Gallery, 3310 Comox Road, Courtenay; (250) 339-7702; www. ihosgallery.com.*
Spirits Of The West Coast Native Art Gallery; 2926 Back Road, Courtenay; (250) 338-2120; spiritsofthewestcoast.com.
K'ómoks First Nation: http://www.comoxband.ca/. Operates a riverfront RV campground seasonally on its Puntledge land.

60 | Cumberland

Cumberland is an attractive, slow-paced community that is reinventing itself as a outdoor recreation centre and small-town residential enclave after a long career as a coal-mining town.

The oldest municipality in the Comox Valley (established 1888), Cumberland was a hard-working city of 3,000, not including Asian miners relegated to outlying swamps. At one time eight mines produced coal, and 18 kilometres of railway carried it to tidewater at Union Bay. The whole enterprise, including the town, was a Dunsmuir family project.

Since the last mine shut down in 1966, Cumberland has devolved into a village while the population has actually increased (3,163 est 2009). The core area of 30 blocks retains a good stock of heritage buildings among more recent constructions. There is a modest commercial zone on Dunsmuir Ave, although the nearest supermarket is in Courtenay (8 km).

Cumberland has arguably the best hostel on the island — certainly the best named. The Riding Fool Hostel occupies a nicely redone 1895 commercial building. There's a spacious lounge with a pool table.

You can rent bikes from the shop on the street and pick up maps of the area's extensive network of mountain bike trails.

Up the way is the Waverley Hotel bar, legendary for live music and crowds from Mt Washington. The Waverley Hotel opened in 1894 as a temperance — anti-booze — boarding house. The Wave has been serving drinks since the 1920s.

The nearby Cumberland Museum and Archives celebrates the valley's coal-mining heritage. Outstanding exhibits simulate the work in the mines and the life of the town. The museum's excellent website is crammed with photos and narratives of the old days. A fascinating thread outlines the intricate structure of Cumberland's Chinatown, once one of BC's largest.

A forward-looking group, the Cumberland Community Forest Society, is fundraising the purchase of private forestland surrounding the village. So far, they've raised about $1 million and bought some 60 hectares of second-growth forest. It is now a municipal park. The group's target for the Cumberland Community Forest is 263 hectares.

Details: *The Riding Fool Hostel, 2705 Dunsmuir Ave, Cumberland, 1-888-313-FOOL/(250) 336-8250; http://www.ridingfool.com/. Dorm $23, private room $60. Waverley Hotel, 2692 Dunsmuir Ave, Cumberland; (250) 336-8322: http://waverleyhotel.ca/.*

Cumberland Museum and Archives, 2680 Dunsmuir Ave, Cumberland, (250) 336-2445; http://www.cumberlandmuseum.ca/cgi-bin/show_home.cgi.

Cumberland Community Forest Society: http://www.cumberlandforest.com/index.php.

Comox Valley Mountain Biking: http://www.cvmtb.com/.

Forbidden Plateau 61

Mount Washington, the island's premier alpine sport centre, 33 kilometres west of Courtenay, is known for snow, and it's also a popular summer destination for hikers. Paradise Meadows, Mt Washington's cross-country ski area, is the gateway to the sublime alpine reaches of Strathcona Provincial Park. The 12,400-hectare Forbidden Plateau area was added to the park in 1967.

Trails wind around little lakes in the exquisite subalpine meadows of Forbidden Plateau, between 1,050 and 1,200 metres in elevation. Despite its name, Forbidden Plateau is actually quite ridged and inclined. There are three camping areas to choose from in this enchanting landscape of subalpine spruce and fir trees.

The plateau gives way to the glacier-girt peak of Mount Albert Edward (elevation 2,094 m). The ascent onto the treeless alpine slopes can be hard work, especially the steep climb onto the ridge east of Albert Edward. For a fit hiker with a day-pack, the climb takes as little as 6 hours one-way from the Paradise Meadows park entrance. For the average hiker, it's a three-day trip, with a camp at Circlet Lake. Best time to climb Albert Edward is mid-summer.

The Strathcona Provincial Park Wilderness Centre at Paradise Meadows provides back-country travelers with current information (summer only).

For skiers the peak of Mt Washington, 1,588 m above sea level, overlooks 60 downhill runs and trails — nearly half for advanced skiers/boarders — dropping 505 m and blanketed by snow that averages more than 10 m annually.

The two high-speed lifts stay open for summer mountain bikers, who can choose from 37 km of trails.

Details: *Mount Washington Alpine Resort: http://www.mountwashington.ca/ Staying on the mountain: the pleasant subalpine village has a peak population of 4,000. Walk/ski-in accommodations can be booked through Central Reservations: 1-888-231-1499. The downhill and cross-country lodges have food service in season. Grocery shopping is limited; liquor outlet, gas station.*

Reading: *Guidebook:* Hiking Trails 3: Northern Vancouver Island, *10th edition, 2008. Forbidden Plateau trail map: http://www.env.gov.bc.ca/bcparks/explore/park-pgs/strath/strath_forbidden_area.pdf.*

DELLA FALLS, FROM A VINTAGE POSTCARD (AUTHOR'S COLLECTION)

Southwest Vancouver Island

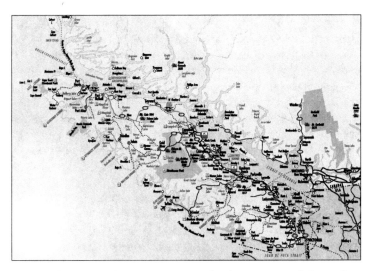

Wet, windswept southwest Vancouver Island presents a rainforest face to the open Pacific along a coast so varied — the Alberni Inlet indents more than half way across the island, while on the West Coast Trail the sandstone shelf is a regular kerb. The west coast has been a forestry supply centre since the first sawmill started in the Alberni valley more than a century ago, and about 40,000 people live in the quarter now. Impossibly colourful west coast towns — Tofino, Ulcuelet, Bamfield and Port Renfrew — are jumping-off points for the wild island. A scary stretch known as the Graveyard of the Pacific provided the impetus for a lifesaving installation that bequeathed us the celebrated West Coast Trail. It and the grandly wild Clayoquot Sound have become wilderness travel destinations known the world over.

62 The West Coast Road

Beyond Sooke the narrow West Coast Road (Highway 14) curls around little coves with pebble beaches. There are more spruce and hemlock trees, fewer Douglas fir. The tang of the open ocean becomes stronger.

Between Shirley and Port Renfrew, a distance of 55 kilometres, we're in forestry country, a land of many trees and few people. The shoulders of the mountains begin to slope right into the sea. Spectacular views unfold.

A drive on the West Coast Road is the easiest way to gain an experience of the island's wild side.

Notable stops along the way:

French Beach, 19 km west of Sooke, has an excellent provincial campground. Gravelly shallows just offshore is a good place to see Gray whales in spring.

Point No Point Resort, Km 22, has 25 well-appointed cabins ranged along the beach. Meals are served in a charming tea house that commands sweeping views of the coast and the straits. It was built by Evelyn Packham, the original proprietor. Miss Packham used to serve tea. Dine there and you gain access to the scenic point, with its curious log bridge.

Jordan River, Km 29, is a logging centre and the site of a 170-mw hydroelectric generating station built 1911. There's good winter surfing off the mouth of the Jordan River. Across the road, a café, a burger shack, and a gas station. The views across the Strait of Juan de Fuca are spectacular.

China Beach, Km 35, is the eastern terminus of the Juan de Fuca Trail, which winds along the coast 47 km to Botanical Beach. The trail is accessible (with parking lots) at Sombrio Beach (29 km from China Beach) and Parkinson Creek (37 km). China Beach has a beautiful campground and a day-use area.

Sombrio Beach is a famous surfing area. Until recently the beach was the residence of a legendary community of hippie squatters. The parking lot is in second-growth that was in recent memory a magnificent forest of old-growth Sitka spruce.

Details: *French Beach Provincial Park: http://www.env.gov.bc.ca/bcparks/explore/parkpgs/french_bch/.*
Point No Point Resort, 10829 West Coast Road, Shirley; (250) 646-2020; http://www.pointnopointresort.com/.
Juan De Fuca Marine Trail: http://www.env.gov.bc.ca/bcparks/explore/parkpgs/juan_de_fuca/.
Stretches of beach hiking that require knowledge of tides and an eye-out for orange balls that mark trails.

Botanical Beach 63

Botanical Beach, on the open coast near Port Renfrew, is an area famous for tidepools. The pools are created by erosion of flat sandstone shelves that are located between high and low tides — covered at high tide but exposed at low. Tidepools are microcosms of ocean life, of dazzling variety, brimful of pale green anemones, little darting fish, crustaceans hiding in the eelgrass.

More than 100 species of invertebrates and 231 species of plants have been counted in the tidepools of Botanical Beach. It's worth a special trip (a two-hour drive from Victoria) to peer into these cauldrons of ocean life. Just be sure to time your visit to coincide with an ebbing tide, 1.2 metres or lower. And mind you don't stick your hand in the pools — contamination could be lethal to some tidepool denizens.

Sea urchins play an important role in tidepool formation. Geologist Chris Yorath writes: "The extraordinary erosive power of sea urchins . . . has yet to be appreciated by geologists." Many pools are exquisitely shaped, with smooth vertical sides, often honeycombed with purple sea urchins, each in its own circular recess, slowly eroding the rock with its five teeth, enlarging the pool.

During one visit to Botanical Beach, I watched a small fish jump out of a tidepool and flip-flop across the flat sandstone, pursued by a tiny octopus. Guess it couldn't stand the thought of waiting for the next tide. The octopus barely glanced at the ring of visitors, who were staring at it slack-jawed.

The place was discovered in 1900 by Josephine Tilden, a biologist who had recently earned her Master of Science degree at the University of Minnesota and was the first woman professor in science there. A native of Iowa, Tilden located Botanical Beach by canoe. She invested her own capital to help establish the Minnesota Seaside Station, the first marine biology research facility on the northwest coast.

A profile on the university's website sketches the scene at Botanical Beach:

Up to 30 professors and students journeyed to the station . . . every summer to study geology, algology, zoology, taxonomy, and lichenology; world-renowned scientists participated in the lecture series. . . Letters from student Alice Misz to her mother during the summer of 1906 make it clear that her six-week stay at the station was the most unforgettable experience of her life.

The station closed in 1907 — the university declined to continue supporting it.

Josephine Tilden (1869-1957) never took a doctorate, but she became a renowned authority on algae. *The Algae and Their Life Relations: Fundamentals of Phycology* (1935) is still in print.

Protected in a provincial park since 1989, with 331 hectares of upland and 120 ha of foreshore, Botanical Beach is now part of Juan de Fuca Provincial Park. It's the western terminus of the highly scenic but still very rough Juan de Fuca Marine Trail. Much of Botanical Beach itself is rough walking across broken terrain.

The network of trails around Botanical Beach includes a circuit by way of a short, scenic trail west to Botany Bay, where the geological history of the region is written in the rocks.

Details: *Botanical Beach parking lot is 3 km S of Port Renfrew; then an easy walk through young forest less than 1 km.*

Juan de Fuca Provincial Park: http://www.env.gov.bc.ca/bcparks/explore/park-pgs/juan_de_fuca/.

64 Big Trees of San Juan Valley

The largest Douglas fir tree in the world and the largest Sitka spruce tree in Canada can be seen in a day trip to the San Juan Valley near Port Renfrew.

Little visited because of the turbulent terrain and isolation of the San Juan Valley, the Red Creek Fir and the San Juan Spruce are not difficult to find, and they are on the same route. But the approach is by four-wheel-drive vehicle only — spare tires, jacks and tire inflation kits are a must.

These giants beggar description. Their massive trunks are draped with ferns and epiphytes. The first branches are higher than most trees. One has monster forks and strange deformities. Their size and undoubted great age inspire awe.

The Red Creek Fir is 73.8 metres high and 13.28 m in circumference; its crown spreads 22.8 m. Its total volume is estimated at 349 cu m. It's not just the largest known Douglas fir — it's the largest known tree in the entire family of Pinaceae, which includes many conifers (pines, spruces, true firs, hemlocks and larches as well as Douglas fir).

The San Juan Spruce is 62.5 m high and has a circumference of 11.66 m, with a crown that spreads 23 m. Its total volume is estimated to be 333 cu m, making it the second largest known Sitka spruce and the third largest Pinacea. (The Queets spruce in Washington's Olympic Peninsula is bigger.)

The record holders are the remnant of a population of superbig trees that once inhabited the Pacific coast. There's evidence that Douglas fir trees grew as tall as 125 m on the island — likely through a combination of super genes, superproductive microsites and tenacity.

A special breed of adventurer prowls the back country looking for giant trees. The Ancient Forest Alliance (AFA) is carrying on the work of A.C. Carder and Randy Stoltmann, publishing photos of Vancouver Island's amazing giant trees and stumps on the internet. The Red Creek Fir and the San Juan Spruce, like most giant trees, languish unknown and unvisited, utterly unprotected, on public land, in active logging zones. There's a whole forest of giant redcedars in the logging-threatened Avatar Grove in the nearby Gordon River valley.

The group is trying to halt logging of endangered old-growth on the island and promote sustainable logging of second-growth forests instead.

Details: *Directions to the San Juan Spruce and Red Creek Fir, Avatar Grove other big trees and old-growth forests: www.ancientforestguide.com.*

The Vancouver Island Backroad Mapbook *(5th ed 2008) is the greatest help in finding these areas.*

Photo gallery of big trees and stumps: http://www.ancientforestalliance.org/galleries.php.
Register of Big Trees in British Columbia: http://www.for.gov.bc.ca/hre/bigtrees/docs/BigTreeRegistry.pdf.

Reading: Giant Trees of Western North America and the World *by Al Carder (Harbour, 2005).*

West Coast Trail	65

The West Coast Trail is 75 kilometres of up and down — down yet another endless ladder and up another — across, over, under, around, through — slithering through openings that snag your 20-kilogram pack and leave you wriggling like a turtle.

In return you get seascapes that give you a feeling of being present at the Creation. You feel fresh and new beside big mother Pacific. Its breathing wakes you up in the larger sense. The crashing surf and vivid sea smells are your constant companions, whether you're on the forest trail or walking the beach or the sandstone shelf. Equally in-your-nose are the rank smells of a fallen log turning to soil. You'll see the remnants of annual rings peeking out of a mound of bright red humus.

A sandstone shelf stretches along the shore of much of the southern half. The sandstone shelf is one of the most amazing landforms I've ever seen. It's the most notable landscape of the Trail, in the Not To Be Missed category.

The shelf, at times hundreds of metres wide, always flat as a pancake, occupies the intertidal zone. It's exposed at low tide, covered at high. With a map and current tide tables, you can calculate when it's okay to walk the shelf, where to get down off the trail and, more important, where to get back up.

There are many scenic highlights along the Trail — Tsusiat Falls, the cliffs north of Nitinat Narrows, the old-growth forest between Nitinat and Clo-ose, the pebble beaches near Carmanah Point, to name a few.

Having hiked the West Coast Trail both ways, I recommend first-timers start at Pachena Bay, at the northwest (Bamfield) end. You get the easy part at the beginning and a long climb to the height-of-land near the end.

Some people beginning at the Gordon River (Port Renfrew) avoid the big climb by hiring a boat to take them to Thrasher Cove (where there's a really long ladder climb) and even Owen Point, which shortens the trip by a day and puts you right on the shelf.

The trail has been improved with boardwalks, bridges and cable car crossings that have tamed some of the more rugged bits. Still, you don't trifle with the trail. You mustn't mind being wet. It might rain for six days and six nights, even in summer. Plan accordingly. Be strategic. Take lots of socks. But go. Allow at least six days. Research the campsites.

Details: *The West Coast Trail is part of the Pacific Rim Park Reserve of Canada and is open May-Sept. Parks Canada (www.pc.gc.ca) requires all users to purchase passes and take an orientation. The points of access are Pachena Bay (Bamfield) and Gordon River (Port Renfrew). You can leave at Nitinat Lake, but you can't enter there. Access is restricted to a daily quota. During high season, visitors can reserve a start time (90-day lead; fee) or show up and wait for openings. Private First Nations operators provide crossings at Gordon River and Nitinat (fees). A shuttle service from Victoria and Nanaimo drops and picks up hikers (www.trailbus.com). A leisurely scenic approach is via the coaster MV Frances Barkley between Port Alberni and Bamfield.*

66 Nitinat

Nitinat Lake is famous for the westerly winds that rise every morning like clockwork from April to September. The winds, strong and steady, make Nitinat a top North American destination among superathletic windsurfers and kiteboarders.

From afar you see the taut sails cutting back and forth across the lake. Less than 2 kilometres wide, the lake is 23 km long from the outlet of the Nitinat River to the mouth of Nitinat Narrows. Nitinat Lake is a finger of ocean — the tides fairly rip through the 40-metre-wide narrows.

For the most of us who don't do high-energy windsurfing, Nitinat is the portal to Carmanah-Walbran Park and the West Coast Trail.

This is the traditional domain of the Ditidaht First Nation. A visitor centre at the north end of Nitinat Lake has a café, store, gas station and small motel. There's a campground, popular in summer, on the lake. The Ditidaht people are also boat operators for West Coast Trail hikers crossing Nitinat Narrows.

For those inclined to poke around, a visit to the Cheewhat Lake Cedar is a must. It's a 20- to 40-minute hike off the Rosander Main, the logging road that leads to the Carmanah Valley. The trail is rough and poorly marked. The reward is to stand next to the largest known tree in Canada — a western redcedar 18.34 m in circumference and 55.5 m tall, with a 15.6 m spread and an estimated volume of 449 cu m. Estimates of the age of the vast, still growing, conifer range up to 2,500 years.

A place that's good to know about, but don't feel you have to go there, is the Nitinat Triangle, a rugged area of small lakes and old-growth forest on the west side of Nitinat Lake. Protected in the 1970s, when the area was added to Pacific Rim National Park, the triangle is renowned among wilderness trekkers.

A combination of paddling and grueling portages puts one at the head of beautiful Tsusiat Falls, above the West Coast Trail. The hardcore rope their vessels and supplies down to the trail, launch into the chuck from the sandstone shelf (highly dangerous) and paddle through Nitinat

TAKE5 STAR WEISS'S FIVE
SACRED PLACES

Victoria author Star Weiss, a native of New York, has lived up and down Vancouver Island for more than 30 years.

I am fascinated by the power of place on the west coast, and by the locations British Columbians choose as havens. Here are five sacred places from my book *Havens in a Hectic World: Finding Sacred Places* (Touchwood Editions, 2008; see www. starweiss.ca).

1. **Yuquot**
Ancient home of the Mowachaht people on Nootka Island. One of the most spiritual places in BC — mystical, historical. Accessible via the *Uchuck III* from Gold River.

2. **Congregation Emanu-El, Victoria**
Oldest surviving synagogue on the west coast, now a National Historic Site, restored to its former beauty; tours can be arranged.

3. **Providence Farm, Duncan**
A place of compassion and inclusiveness, sacred to the Quw'utsun people, now well-known for its horticultural therapy program. Sits on a beautiful 400 acres — a magical setting.

4. **Mt. Albert Edward, Forbidden Plateau**
This is my church, halfway to heaven, a place where I feel close to the divine — accessible via the Paradise Meadows trail at Mt. Washington.

5. **Carmanah-Walbran Provincial Park**
A mystical spot where, as Leonard Cohen wrote, "God is alive, magic is afoot." It is the forest primeval. You'll feel like a tree-elf standing among the ancient giants. Worth the daunting trip to get there.

Narrows (ditto). The more sensible rope their stuff down and then wait for a Ditidaht water taxi to transport them through the Narrows. The circuit is 38 km and requires 3-5 days.

Details: *Nitinat Lake is usually approach from the east side via Youbou or Port Alberni, on logging roads. A scenic route from Victoria follows the West Coast Road to Port Renfrew, the Harris Creek Road to Cowichan Lake and the South Shore Rd to the Nitinat Main. Either way, logging road travel is involved.*
Ditidaht First Nation: http://www.ditidaht.ca/.
Cheewhat Lake Cedar: Roadside parking at N 48° 41.562, W 124° 44.154; site at N 48° 41.7, W 124° 44.376. The tree is within the boundary of Pacific Rim Park, but the road isn't.

Carmanah Walbran 67

The old-growth forest in Carmanah-Walbran, south of Lake Cowichan and west of Port Renfrew, is a world of perpetual shade broken by shafts of light, of profound silences punctuated by birdsong… the creaking of ancient wood… the plash of water on creekrock. The provincial park, established between 1990 and 1995, protects 16,450 ha of west-coast rainforest in the adjacent valleys of Carmanah, Walbran, Logan and Cullite creeks.

Access to Carmanah is via Cowichan and Nitinat lakes and the Rosander Main, through areas of active logging. Be prepared to meet — and know how to avoid — logging trucks. The trailhead is about four hours from Victoria.

First-time visitors head for the Three Sisters, a 2.5 km hike upriver, and the Randy Stoltmann Commemorative Grove, 2.6 km downstream. Stoltmann, a tireless advocate for ancient forests, brought Carmanah into the public eye in 1988. There are three small campgrounds in the valley.

The Carmanah Giant, at 96 m the tallest known tree in Canada and believed the third tallest Sitka spruce anywhere, is growing in a ravine near the bottom of the lower Carmanah Trail, which is officially closed.

Approaches to the larger and equally interesting Walbran Valley requires a Left fork after the Caycuse Bridge. Best access is via McClure Main and Glad Lake Main.

Logging companies have been working in the 7,500-ha Upper Walbran for years, and you will find many a cedar stump of 5 metres diameter. But much of the Upper Walbran is still clothed in old-growth forest.

The bridge on Walbran Creek near the park boundary makes a fine destination for car camping and day trips. The Upper Walbran has some good trails, some with boardwalks, stairs, bridges and gorgeous river-side campsites.

Not far from the bridge is Castle Grove, one of the best remaining old-growth redcedar forests on the island. Nearby swimming holes

TAKE 5 BRUCE WHITTINGTON'S FIVE
EXCELLENT BIRDING ADVENTURES

Freelance naturalist, writer and photographer Bruce Whittington is author of three books, most recently What's That Island? — a guide to the 90-minute BC Ferry crossing between Tsawwassen and Swartz Bay. He leads interpretive cruises to such special places as Haida Gwaii. A longtime resident of Victoria, Bruce now makes his home in Ladysmith.

1. Herring spawn
Early in spring the herring spawn along the east coast of the island. The water takes on a milky colour. The spectacle attracts many species of wildlife, including numbers of sea lions and thousands upon thousands of seabirds that feed on the herring and their roe. But it's hard to know where the herring will appear. One way is to follow the herring fishery. The fishboats get short openings on short notice. You have to ask around.

2. Raptor migration
One of my favorite birding spots is a rocky promontory in East Sooke Park I call Hawk Lookout. I like to sit up on the rocks on a nice September day and watch the Turkey Vultures stage their annual migration across the Strait of Juan de Fuca, joined by as many as a dozen other species of raptors.

3. Active Pass
On the Swartz Bay-Tsawwassen ferry route through the Gulf Islands, this Important Bird Area (IBA) is especially interesting during migration times, when you will see thousands of Bonaparte Gulls and Pacific Loons that stop to refuel for the next leg of their travels.

4. Pelagic birding
On these boating excursions from west coast ports — Port Renfrew, Bamfield, Ucluelet or Tofino — you travel 50 km or more offshore. You're in a wilderness where you see Black-footed Albatrosses and several species of shearwaters, birds that travel huge distances without ever setting foot on land except to breed.

5. Saanich Peninsula
Wintering birds, including waterfowl and the raptors that feed on them, gather in the Martindale Valley, along with the vagrant species that set birders' hearts aflutter. The Victoria Christmas Day Bird Count consistently records more than 100 species in the valley, including a lot of individual rare birds and some spectacular native species — Snowy Owls and Gyrfalcons — you don't often see.

include Walbran Falls, with tiered waterfalls and deep pools, a 15-minute walk upriver.

BC Parks' map warns that the Lower Walbran is *potentially unsafe* and *discourages access*. I've hiked a ways down the Walbran creekbed from the bridge. It's a miracle of geologic diversity and great beauty.

Details: *Carmanah Walbran Provincial Park: http://www.env.gov.bc.ca/bcparks/ explore/parkpgs/carmanah/. Has map and directions to Carmanah. Walbran Creek bridge: GPS lat 48.650887, long -124.593415.*

68 Bamfield and Barkley Sound

Bamfield is a quaint fishing village with arms on either side of little Banfield Inlet, near Barkley Sound. Access to the west side of Bamfield is by water. A boardwalk runs between the houses and the tide. Front doors open off the boardwalk. The docks are roofless garages for the family speedboat. Get moving, Junior — better not miss the school boat.

This charming sea-drenched place is right next door to two huge semi-wilderness experiences — Barkley Sound and the West Coast Trail.

Bamfield itself is still relatively isolated, with logging road access from Cowichan Lake and Port Alberni. Or there's a half-day cruise to Bamfield aboard the packet freighter *Francis Barkley*. The approach by sea is highly recommended.

The freighter's base is a dock near the foot of Argyle St, main street of old Port Alberni. Spacious Argyle St has a partially-preserved old-town streetscape. Harbour Quay is a People Place of shops, a museum, an heritage railway locomotive and lots of open space. There are splendid views of the head of Alberni Canal and the spacious Alberni Valley. The forestry town, area pop 25,297 (2006), is economically reduced from its heyday, but it retains a paper mill, a sawmill and a deep-sea port.

Make sure to get the right day: the boat sails to Bamfield on Tuesdays, Thursdays and Saturdays year 'round (4½ hours one way) and in the summer Sundays, with a turn through the Broken Group on the outbound (5½ hr). On other days the freighter goes to Ucluelet.

The cruise down 40-kilometre-long Alberni Canal — longest of many fjords on the Island — is scenic enough, but save your batteries for the gorgeous vistas of Barkley Sound.

The most open of the island's five *sounds*, Barkley Sound is 24 km wide and indented as much as 25 km, not including Alberni Canal. *Sound* is a misnomer — these sounds are not passages but whole complexes of *inlets*.

Kayakers bound for the Broken Group do not cross the open water from Bamfield unless they are storm-hardened Eskimo-rollers. The highly scenic Deer Group of Islands is much nearer, and there's a put-in near the Centennial Park campground on Port Desire, Bamfield East. Many campsites are perilously close to high tide — but on the other hand the Deer Group has relatively few visitors to its sea caves and sparkling white beaches.

(More on access to the Broken Group under Ucluelet.)

Bamfield is blessed with remarkably surroundings. Across the little peninsula of Bamfield West is exquisite Brady's Beach. Along the same coast is *Kiix?in* (Keeshan), ancient fortified village of the Nuu-chah-nulth people — now a National Historic Site of Canada.

On the eastern slope of Banfield Inlet is the Bamfield Marine Sciences Centre, a renowned university-level centre of field and training that offers tours to summer visitors. The tanks of local sealife are eye-popping.

The site was long occupied by a Cable Station, connected by a single 4000-km-long underwater telegraph cable with Fanning Id, Fiji. It was one lap in the round-the-world telecommunications system known as the All Red Route — so named because routed entirely through British possessions. At the cable station the barely perceptible clicks of faraway telegraph machines would be amplified, picked up by batteries of head-phoned clerks and relayed to Port Alberni.

Details: *Lady Rose Marine Services, 5425 Argyle Street, Port Alberni, next to Alberni Harbour Quay; (250) 723-8313 (year 'round during office hours) 1-800-663-7192 (summer): http://www.ladyrosemarine.com/rates.html.*
Bamfield Marine Sciences Centre: http://www.bms.bc.ca/.
Bamfield directory of accommodations and amenities: http://www.bamfield-chamber.com/directory.html.

Bamfield Coast Guard Station　69

The province's oldest lifeboat station (established 1908) occupies the picturesque grassy grounds and white heritage buildings of the Canadian Coast Guard base in Bamfield West. It had the world's first purpose-built power lifeboat.

The lifesaving station was established after the wreck of the SS *Valencia* in 1906. The same disaster sparked construction of the Pachena Point lighthouse and the West Coast Lifesaving Trail.

The coast of Vancouver Island on either side of Barkley Sound is known as the Graveyard of the Pacific.

The craggy shores east of Bamfield form one side of the funnel that is the Strait of Juan de Fuca. The strait is a major shipping channel to ports at Vancouver, Point Roberts, Seattle and Tacoma and dozens of smaller ports around the so-called Salish Sea.

The coast is pounded by the frigid Pacific and lashed by howling win-ter winds. It's one of the wildest stretches anywhere.

Beneath lie dozens of ships' hulls. More than a few travelers have found a watery grave there.

Many an approaching ship was driven onto the rocks during storms. If you were bearing north along the Washington coast, and you missed the Cape Flattery Light — marking the entrance to Juan de Fuca Strait — you might continue north until the dreaded cry went up: "Breakers ahead!"

The Cape Beale Lighthouse was built at the southern entrance of Barkley Sound in 1874 to guide ships in and out. The lightkeepers saved lives — as when in 1906 Minnie Patterson slogged 10 km through swamps in the teeth of a howling December storm to summon the survey vessel *Quadra* from Bamfield. It was able to rescue all aboard a ship that had swamped near the cape.

The Carmanah Point Lighthouse was built in 1891 to help ships find the entrance of Juan de Fuca Strait.

In January 1906, the SS *Valencia* was carrying nearly 180 passengers and crew from San Francisco to Seattle when it missed the entrance of the strait and ran onto a reef near Pachena Point. The captain disengaged it, then ran it on the rocks again to avoid sinking.

As the storm raged, huge waves ripped people off the decks. Lifeboats spilled the occupants into the ocean. Some made it to shore only to be plucked off the rocks. Those who struggled up the cliffs encountered impenetrable thickets of salal.

Survivors found the Cape Beale Lighthouse and summoned rescuers who flocked to the ship by land and sea, only to discover they could do nothing but watch.

They saw women lashed to masts with their children to avoid being swept away, calling for help until succumbing to hypothermia.

Only 37 survived — all adult males.

Rarely has Canadian public opinion changed political wills as quickly as when the news of the *Valencia* disaster hit the wires.

Today a fleet of 14 vessels, two hovercraft, 16 search and rescue lifeboats and five helicopters patrols the Graveyard of the Pacific. The Bamfield station has a staff of four and two lifesaving boats.

Part of the vital work of the Bamfield Coast Guard is looking out for the safety of the waterborne visitors to Barkley Sound and hikers on the West Coast Trail.

The rescue coordination centre in Victoria responds to more than 2,100 maritime search-and-rescue calls annually, of which about one-fifth are people in distress. Rapid responses by the Coast Guard save an estimated 1,400 lives a year.

Details: *Graveyard of the Pacific, an interesting website: http://www.pacificship-wrecks.ca/english/index.html*
Minnie Patterson, Cape Beale Lighthouse keeper who saved the Coloma: http://www.lighthousefriends.com/light.asp?ID=1199.

70 Sproat Lake Water Bombers

Two gigantic forest fire-fighting water-bombers are based on Sproat Lake, a scenic resort near Port Alberni. Cottagers have front row seats for a spectacle often repeated during busy fire seasons.

A red and white Martin Mars lumbers in over the treetops, skims along the lake at 70 knots, scooping up water — 27,000 kilograms a load — then climbs to some distant fire site to drop a 1.6-hectare wet blanket of water mixed with flame-retarding foam. This they can repeat every 15 minutes.

The Martin Mars is a World War II-era US Navy long-range transport aircraft — the largest of the *flying boats* and the largest functioning airplane until the B-36 (1947). Two Mars were acquired by a consortium of BC forestry companies and adapted to carrying water. A fixture on Sproat Lake since 1960, and now owned by Coulson, a Port Alberni firm, the water bombers have fought many a forest fire on Vancouver Island — and elswhere.

In 2009 one of the Mars, on lease to the US Forest Service, helped fight the 127,000-acre Station Fire near Los Angeles. The Mars and its big wet blanket is credited with saving the historic Wilson Observatory.

Sproat Lake Provincial Park is virtually next door to the tanker base. The 43-hectare park has both a day use area with good swimming and two campgrounds. It's a good places to watch the show — but there's no schedule.

Details: *Coulson Flying Tankers: http://www.martinmars.com/.*
Sproat Lake Provincial Park: http://www.env.gov.bc.ca/bcparks/explore/parkpgs/ sproat_lk/. Turnoff 12 km west of Port Alberni on Route 4.
There are also rustic lodgings along Lakeshore Rd.

Della Falls 71

Della Falls is a grand spectacle on the remote southern edge of Strathcona Park, where Drinkwater Creek tumbles off a towering rampart of rock.

Della Falls drops, cascades over rocks, then drops again. The falls and cascades total 440 metres, making Della Falls the tallest waterfall in Canada — officially. The relative lengths of the segments have been triangulated as about 4:1:2.

That was its state when I stood at base of the falls. During heavy rains, observers report, Della Falls becomes one long arc.

There are several ways to approach Della Falls, all on foot. From the north it's possible to drop into the subalpine valley via extremely rugged trails from Bedwell Lake or Cream Lake.

The only access from below is by way of the moderately challenging trail up Drinkwater Creek.

Getting to the trailhead can be a challenge in itself. It's at the west end of Great Central Lake. The lake is only traversable by boat, about a 35-km trip. If you are self-propelled, it's important to know the lake can be inhospitable. Never mind finding a campsite — there's virtually no place to land. Winds can blow up in the afternoon and make a hell of paddling.

There is an alternative — hire powerboat transport at the Ark Resort or through a Port Alberni outfitter.

Even with the motor assist, a trip to Della Falls requires at least one night of camping. There are campsites along the trail of varying dampness. If you're paddling, allow 3 to 5 nights.

It's a 7-hour hike to the base of the falls. The vertical gain is about 500 m, mostly in the last third. There are three crossings. The bridge at Km 11 has been disabled for some time, making improvised crossings necessary.

(BC Parks is installing a cable car crossing at Km 11, completion expected by September 2010. Meantime, BC Parks' Strathcona Park website advises the trail is closed. Yet I hear reports of successful hikes. Go figure.)

For a view of the falls from above, plan to climb an extra 3 hours up to Love Lake. The switchback trail gains 800 m altitude and is best undertaken by experienced hikers without full packs. There are several lookouts en route to charming Love Lake.

Della Falls — getting there is more than half the fun.

(Is Della Falls really the highest waterfall in Canada? Contrarians think they have discovered higher falls on northern Vancouver Island. Kiwi Falls in Schoen Lake Provincial Park is estimated to be 480 m. An unnamed falls at the head of Woss Lake, about 500 m.)

Details: *Ark Resort, 11000 Central Lake Rd, Port Alberni, (250) 723-2657; http://www.arkresort.com/. Will rent canoes. No credit cards. Website has trail reports.*
Guidebook: Hiking Trails 3: Northern Vancouver Island, 10th edition, 2008. Detailed coverage and maps of trails around Della Falls.
Atlas of Canada tallest waterfall list: atlas.nrcan.gc.ca/site/english/learningresources/facts/waterfalls.html.

72	Ucluelet

The oceanside village of Ucluelet (pronounced *You CLUE lit* and often *You CUE lit*) enjoys a splendid situation on a spectacular section of west coast. It straddles a rocky peninsula just west of the entrance of Barkley Sound, south of Clayoquot Sound and east of Long Beach.

Ucluelet, pop 1,591 (2009 est), was not that long ago a lunchbucket town, a rough-edged service centre for the logging industry. To get there you drove through a moonscape. Politically it was Tofino's opposite. The moonscape has greened up, the loggers have moved on, and Ucluelet has become a destination in its own right.

The town's most notable feature is its highly scenic broken outer coast. The 12-km Wild Pacific Trail gives you a taste of that, in three easily-accessible sections. The oceanside trail is being extended westward to Pacific Rim National Park.

Ucluelet is the terminus of the packet freighter *Francis Barkley* from Port Albeni. The passenger carrier links Ucluelet with the beauties of Barkley Sound Mondays, Wednesdays and Fridays, June to mid-September.

The Broken Group of Islands are nearby. Myriad tiny islets and reefs line the channels. Camping is excellent on the seven designated islands in the Broken Group but beware — the tiny archipelago gets busy by mid-summer. You can be dropped off in your kayak. Be sure to book transport for your craft well in advance.

(For more about MV *Francis Barkley*, see Bamfield.)

Ucluelet itself is a dangerous place to launch kayaks for a crossing — the open water can become dangerous to small craft without warning at any time of year. Kayakers launch for the Broken Group from Toquart Bay, on the west side of the sound, with a campground and store. Or they rent from Seshart Lodge, on the Francis Barkley's route. (See ladyrosemarine.com for more information.) Or they go in a group excursion with a wilderness kayaking outfit.

Ucluelet's wildlife touring and whale watching businesses have grown enormously. Among many attractions are spring and fall migrations of Gray whales and humpback whales between southern and northern waters.

Sport salmon fishing, a mainstay of local enterprise, goes from U-rent to the spiffy Canadian Princess Resort, where you can stay aboard an heritage yacht and go out for guided day trips.

Details: *Ucluelet lodgings and amenities: http://www.uclueletinfo.com/visitor_ information/default.htm.*
Wild Pacific Trail: http://www.longbeachmaps.com/wildtrail.html.
Pacific Rim National Park Reserve of Canada, Broken Group Islands camping: http://www.pc.gc.ca/eng/pn-np/bc/pacificrim/activ/activ5b.aspx.
Toquart Bay Campground: reservations (250) 726-8349; http://www.toquartbay. com/campground.html.
Majestic Ocean Kayaking, 1-800-889-7644, or (250) 726-2868;.

Long Beach | 73

Long Beach is the heart of Pacific Rim National Park, established in the 1970s to protect sections of the island's spectacular west coast.

Pacific Rim Park encloses 29,000 hectares of land and 22,000 ha of foreshore in three sections. The Long Beach section includes 30 kilometres of varied coast and nearby old-growth forest between Ucluelet and Tofino on Esowista Peninsula. The other sections are the Broken Group of Islands in Barkley Sound and the West Coast Trail.

Long Beach was a legend for decades before Highway 4 was completed from Port Alberni, and streams of people started to travel the winding road to camp in the west coast wilderness. When Parks Canada moved in, a community of squatters pulled up stakes, but many stuck around, making a go of it on a bit of land or in nearby Tofino. Some are there today.

Long Beach is the centre of a 16-kilometre continuum of sand that is wider than most beaches are long. The scale of it defies description. The roar of the pounding surf is a constant. It rumbles under your feet. The spray resolves into rainbow mists. Depending on the season there's a scene of wetsuited surfers. They grab their boards and vanish into the distances. Some visitors attribute spiritual qualities to Long Beach after experiencing its vast openness.

You come to this spectacle through a curtain of ancient Sitka spruce trees. Their lichen-trailing branches harbour ravens and eagles. Sitka spruce grows well here, even when the roots are lapping in salt water. The standing dead shed their scaly bark to reveal the massive cylinders of the trunks, scored by spiraling fissures.

The splendid Wickaninnish Interpretive Centre is a must-see. There are 12 km of boardwalk and trails through the nearby forests and bogs, with guided tours in season. To camp at Green Point, you'd better reserve during the summer months.

Details: *Pacific Rim National Park Reserve of Canada: http://www.pc.gc.ca/ pn-np/bc/pacificrim/index.aspx. Day-use fees apply.*

| 74 | Clayoquot Sound |

An early English immigrant named Fred Tibbs bought a little island off Tofino — it's the middle of the three islands nearest the 4th St docks. He called it Dreamisle. Others named it Tibbs' Island. Today it's known as Arnet Id.

Tibbs logged the whole island, leaving just one giant spruce. He topped it at 100 feet, limbed it, nailed rungs to the trunk — enclosed the ladder in a framework of 2x6-inch boards bottom to top — and capped it with a 10x10-ft platform. From a distance it looked pretty ghastly. A bit of a hermit, Fred would sit there listening to gramophone records or playing his cornet.

Tibbs didn't get Clayoquot Sound. Still, I'd like to have ten minutes on that platform, just to look around.

Clayoquot Sound has a piercing beauty and a wild energy. Whether you're contemplating its vistas of endless sand or the myriad surf-washed islands or the mountains that rise right out of the water, this is Earth at its most dramatically varied. It's a place where sensory stimuli crowd in on you — the exhalations of its mudflats, its fine mists, a passing pod of whales, the eagle's keening cry. There's a lot to take in.

Meares Island dominates the landscape with its two sugarloaf peaks — Mt Colnett (elevation 792 metres) 5 kilometres E and Lone Cone (742 m) 6 km N. The third prominent landmark is Catface Mountain, 13 km NW of Tofino. The three mountains are remarkably alike in shape and wonderfully aligned.

The peaks mark the boundary between the Estevan Lowland and the Vancouver Island Fiordlands.

Outside the line are landscapes exposed to the ocean, hugely composed of sand. Esowista Peninsula and Vargas Id are mostly sand. The lowland is underlain by relatively recent rock formations.

On the inland side are nine inlets and lakes that flow into Clayoquot, along strikingly parallel lines. The longest inlets, Herbert and Bedwell, terminate 30 km from the outside coast. They are true fjords, sculpted by ice, with side walls extending deep into water at the heads.

The inland boundary of Clayoquot is defined by the watersheds that drain into the nine inlets and lakes.

The whole complex of islands and inlets known as Clayoquot Sound is about 100 km across from Kennedy Lake to Hesquiat Peninsula. In all, 350,000 hectares of land and water.

Between Meares's peaks, you can look up Bedwell Inlet towards snowy Mariner Mountain, 36 km distant but still within Clayoquot's boundaries. You're able to look from tidewater into the heart of Vancouver Island.

The Catface Range separates two parts of Clayoquot Sound. Beyond it is Sulphur Passage, the gateway to western Clayoquot Sound. The Megin River, the largest primeval watershed remaining on the island, flows into Shelter Inlet, one of four on that side of Catface.

You can't see any of that from the lookout. Clayoquot is vast, varied, profound.

Readings: Settling Clayoquot *by Bob Bossin (Sound Heritage 1981). Fascinating oral history, including the story of Fred Tibbs.*
Voices from the Sound: Chronicles of Clayoquot Sound and Tofino 1899-1929 *by Margaret Horsfield (Salal Books, 2008).*

Kennedy River Bridge   75

Clayoquot Sound caught the world's attention in the summer of 1993, when some 12,000 people made their way to the Peace Camp in the forestry wasteland Black Hole. They came to put their bodies in the way of the logging trucks at the bottleneck Kennedy River Bridge, point of entry to the area where loggers were working.

The first trucks would appear at about 5 AM. Those who were willing to be arrested blocked the truckers' access to the bridge and refused to move. All were pledged to practice non-violence.

Media attention was already focused on the island's red-hot anti-clearcut logging dispute. At the Kennedy River Bridge it went viral. The protest was also a magnet for logging advocates.

The company obtained court injunctions prohibiting obstruction. The second arrest — when the person was in knowing violation of the injunction — drew criminal contempt charges. The RCMP would confront the defiant and cart another limp body away. On one tumultuous day, August 9, more than 1,000 people gathered, and more than 300 were arrested. It took seven hours to clear the bridge.

In the months that followed, 857 people were tried and convicted in several courts. The sentences included fines as high as $3,000 and as much as six months in prison. The convicted got criminal records.

Why did they do it?

Clayoquot's 264,000 hectares of land comprises about eight percent of the island, but it has six of the island's 17 remaining intact watersheds larger than 5,000 ha. It has the largest area of old-growth forest left on Vancouver Island, and the best, most intact ancient temperate rainforest remaining anywhere.

Clayoquot Sound has been clearcut logged since the 1960s. Steep slopes facing the ocean are particularly prone to *mass wasting* after roading and logging. The long plumes of avalanches become starkly visible as the surroundings green up.

Logging increased dramatically in the 1980s. In 1988, the equivalent of 29,000 truckloads of logs were hauled out of Clayoquot.

Local citizens tried every avenue to get a hearing. Industry and government followed the line of *Talk and Log*. They would invite the public to sit on *teams* and help *plan* the future of the sound, while the trees just fell faster.

In March 1993, the government of the day — the left-leaning NDP — put forward a plan that opened 85 percent of the productive forests of Clayoquot Sound to logging.

Tofino-based Friends of Clayoquot Sound organized the blockade.

"Civil disobedience. . . is a refusal to comply with laws that are perceived as unjust," Ontarian Sheldon Lipsey, one of the convicted, told the court, "in this case, laws that protect a private company's financial interests in cutting down trees but fail to protect the public's interest in preserving this country's natural heritage, as well as land to which the First Nations have never given up title."

One result was that the BC government promised to reform logging to where it would stand up to world scrutiny. A blue-ribbon scientific panel recommended adoption of a valley-by-valley approach to logging and protection of all pristine watersheds. Mapped on Clayoquot Sound's myriad watersheds, the scientific panel's restrictions, strictly applied, would have allowed logging in just 23,000 ha — less than one-tenth.

First Nations firms now own most of the industrial logging rights in Clayoquot Sound. They are logging much less than in the 80s. The rate is now determined by the area. But the companies are logging in pristine watersheds. Iisaak Forest Resources has rights to log 87,000 ha in Clayoquot and Mamook-Coulsen, 49,000 ha. And other companies have logging rights on Crown land. Private forests in Clayoquot, while less extensive, are logged with little regulation of rate or method.

"Most people believe that Clayoquot Sound is saved," said Valerie Langer of Friends of Clayoquot Sound a decade ago. "It is not."

Details: *The Kennedy River Bridge is the point of access to the area the Tla-o-qui-aht First Nation has designated Ha'uukmin Tribal Park, with a protection zone, qwa siin hap (leave as is for now) around the pristine upper Kennedy and Clayoquot river valleys and part of Clayoquot Arm:*
http://wildernesscommittee.org/sites/all/files/publications/2009_clayoquot-sound_web.pdf.
BC Government summaries of 1993 Clayoquot land use decision and initiatives after: http://www.for.gov.bc.ca/dsi/Clayoquot/clayoquot_sound.htm
Clayoquot Sound scientific panel reports: http://www.cortex.org/dow-cla.html
Reading: Clayoquot Mass Trials: Defending the Rainforest, *edited by Ron MacIsaac and Anne Champagne (New Society Publishers, 1994).*
Friends of Clayoquot Sound: http://www.focs.ca/index.asp. Reliable perspectives on local resource issues.

76 Tofino

Approaching Tofino on twisty Highway 4, you get glimpses of the long beaches on one side and the mountains on the other. If you are a first-time visitor and the day is clear, by the time you reach the middle of town you will be utterly gobsmacked. Tofino is possibly the most spectacularly-located town in Canada.

The little fishing village has changed quite a bit since becoming a household name. First it attracted visitors from the long beaches. Then Clayoquot got on the environmental radar. It has become a gateway to wilderness recreation. And a surfing centre. The site of the most urbane wilderness resorts. An upscale cottage enclave. An epicentre of green economic thinkers and doers.

Sociability is part of Tofino's appeal. An annual tide of visitors crests in summer, when the town's population swells from its residential core of 1,829 (2009 est) to the point where it's hard to find a room for the night. Wild youth, whole families in Bermuda shorts, groups of kayakers joggling around in sprayskirts, all prowling Tofino's compact downtown, sucking on lattés and smoothies, queuing at the one supermarket and one laundromat, rubbling shoulders with the locals — First Nations people from nearby villages, the descendants of pioneers, the fisherfolk, the ageing hippies, the weekenders who never left.

It's no paradise. I arrive at my morning hangout, the stone picnic table near the kayak put-in beside the 1st St (Government) wharf. The stone table is a good place to watch the theatre of arrivals and departures at the dock. Dozens of empty bottles and cans litter the site from some buddies' night of carousing. I've noticed a certain amount of public drinking here. Tuff City is a party town.

Tofino has a wholesome side — a sober dedication to social change — that is inspiring. The bank and gas stations are about the only chains. The municipal council recently told McDonald's to take a hike. This is a community with vision.

The nearest point of access to the outer coast is at Tonquin Park. The 12-hectare civic park is a 10-minute walk from the centre of Tofino. A boardwalk leads to a gorgeous sandy beach, broken by outcrops of polished blue rock, facing lively Duffin Passage and green Wikanninnish Island. You may find you're sharing the beach with illicit campers or partyhearties.

Much more popular beaches are McKenzie and Chesterman, between 3.5 and 5 kilometres south of town. A paved sidewalk separates the self-propelled from crazy highway traffic. A funky little shopping centre caters to the surfing crowd.

Details: *Tofino Guide: http://www.tofino-bc.com/.*
Directions to Tonquin Park: Proceed south on 1st St; R on Arnet St, L on Tonquin Park Rd, to end; limited parking.

Meares Island — 77

The two peaks of 8,400-hectare Meares Island overlook Tofino on either side of muddy Lemmens Inlet. The visual centerpiece of Clayoquot Sound is also the most accessible place on Vancouver Island to view an ancient forest.

A short boat ride across Browning Channel and a walk on the boardwalk brings us to the ancient western redcedars. With their dead tops and multiple leaders, the big trees are grotesquely beautiful. While they're not all that tall, they have vast trunks — the largest cedar on the island measures nearly 18 metres in circumference.

These trees are believed to be 1,000 years old or more. They are part of a mixed-species, multigenerational rainforest that is self-perpetuating. Seedlings of spruce, hemlock and cedar take root in the rotting wood of their fallen ancestors, growing in woven shade. We are enfolded by an organism whose strand-entwining roots reach back thousands of years.

Meares owes its pristine character to a blockade that prevented a logging company from gaining entry in 1984. The hereditary chief of the Tla-o-qui-aht First Nation declared Meares Island a tribal park and opened it to visitors, including loggers — without their saws.

Both parties applied for court injunctions to bar the other from the island. First Nations' legal action won the day. Logging was prohibited on Meares pending resolution of First Nations land claims. That's where it stands 25 years later.

I took the invitation to heart. In Lemmens Inlet there are wonderful places to camp. You can watch the eagles play tag while you wait for the tide to return.

Details: *Meares Island Tribal Park and the much larger Ha'uukmin Tribal Park that includes it: http://www.focs.ca/news/2009_clayoquot-sound_web.pdf Meares Island big tree trail water taxi: http://www.oceanoutfitters.bc.ca/meares.htm.*

78 Cultural Adventures

The sea otter trader *Lady Washington*, first seen here in the 1790s, appeared in Clayoquot Sound in July 2005. You couldn't miss its three tiers of gleaming white puffy sails.

The 90-ton replica, out of Grays Harbor, Washington, was here on a mission of reconciliation. A former master of the *Lady*, Captain Robert Gray, was a bit of a hothead, it seems. A descendant came to apologise to First Nations people for Gray's bad behaviour when in the vicinity.

A private ceremony was followed by public celebrations. There was an outdoor feast at Wickaninnish Island, on the ocean side of Tofino. It was a poignant meeting of communities.

The setting was meadowy, just above an amazing hump of sand that stretches through to the ocean side of Wickaninnish, and at high tide separates it from the First Nations island Echachis.

The ship's crew, in nautical costumes, mingled with the local citizens. Teams of local residents bustled about serving dinner.

Contributing the haunches of beef and other food was a social worker from Corvallis, Oregon. William Twombly treats troubled youth and sometimes charters the *Lady Washington* in order to challenge kids via training cruises.

He is the Gray descendant who did the apologizing.

The arrival in Clayoquot Sound of the *Columbia Rediviva*, Robert Gray master, was noted by John Boit, 5th mate:

[August] 29 [1791]. N. Latt. 49° 5´ W. Long. 126° 0´. At Noon the entrance of Clioquot (or Coxes harbour) bore NE 4 leagues. Standing in for the harbour, and towards evening annchor'd in our former station. Vast many of

the Natives along side, and seem'd glad to see us again. found riding here the Brig Lady Washington, of Boston, John Kendrick master, he had made up his Voyage and was bound for Canton. He appear'd happy in meeting with his old friends.

N. Latt 49° 9' W. Long. 125° Captain Kendrick inform'd us that he had had a skirmish with the Natives at Barrells sound (in Queen Charlotte Isles) and was oblidg'd to kill upwards of 50 of them before they wou'd desist from the attack.

On Meares Island, up the east side of Lemmems Inlet, is little Adventure Cove where Gray wintered that year. A painting on glass shows his famous ship *Columbia* with Lone Cone's distinctive silhouette in the background. You won't find a trace of Fort Defiance. Thick mosses cover all.

The First Nations village of Opitsaht has stood on Meares Island since time immemorial. Captain Gray was certain — where others were not — the inhabitants were planning to attack his fort. Having noted the village was empty, Gray sent a force over to burn it. John Boit wrote in his log:

This village was about half a mile in diameter, and contained upwards of 200 Houses, generally well built for Indians; every door that you enter'd was in resemblance to a human and Beast's head, the passage being through the mouth. Besides which there was much more carved work about the dwellings some of which was by no means inelegant. This fine village, the work of Ages, was in a short time totally destroy'd.

The feast was co-hosted by Joe Martin and family, who have a home on Echachis. Joe is a master Tla-o-qui-aht boat carver. A family business, Tla-ook Cultural Adventures, offers paddling tours of Clayoquot Sound in big dugout canoes.

The assembled crowded into a big teepee for some speeches. Joe Martin sang a Nuu-Chah-Nulth song.

The ancient summer village of the Tla-o-qui-aht was at Echachis. It was where the whole nation gathered for offshore fishing and whaling.

I got a sense of how it might be empowering to welcome visitors to your place with generations of ancestors at your side.

Details: *Tla-ook Cultural Adventures, Tofino: (250) 725-2656/1-877-942-2663; http://www.tlaook.com/tlaook-homeset.html.*

The Tonquin Anchor 79

A 3.5-metre-long iron anchor was raised from the bottom of Templar Passage, off Echachis, in 2003. The old anchor retained part of its wooden stock, and glass trade beads were embedded in the metal. It's believed the long-lost anchor of the American fur trader *Tonquin*. The story was familiar to a generation of Americans. Literary heavyweights Washington Irving and Edgar Allen Poe wrote about the *Tonquin*.

Lieutenant Jonathan Thorn, master of the *Tonquin*, a 269-ton barque out of New York, transported the first settlers around Cape Horn to the Pacific Northwest. They were mostly Canadian traders and voyageurs hired by John Jacob Astor to start a fur-trading colony on the Columbia River. The journey was a regular reign of terror. Thorn had a violent temper and sometimes came unhinged. He thought, for example, the Montreal traders were effeminate.

In June 1811 the *Tonquin* set sail from Astoria north to the sea otter coast. The intention was to establish an American fur trade empire based on the China market.

In Clayoquot Sound, Captain Thorn quickly got into an argument with a Tla-o-qui-aht chief and apparently flung some pelts in the chief's face. That was it for the fur trade empire.

The First Nations people returned but when aboard they massacred the captain, the crew, a partner in the Pacific Fur Company and a clerk. Four men escaped in a boat but were soon dispatched. A fifth would not leave the ship. Next day, when the ship was full of plunderers, the fifth survivor ignited the munitions stores. Estimates of First Nations deaths range as high as 200.

There was a survivor among the 27 aboard the *Tonquin*, an interpreter from the Olympic Peninsula known as Joseachal. He was of the Quinault First Nation and had family connections with the Tla-o-qui-aht. Joseachal lived to tell the story back in Astoria.

After that, traders gave Clayoquot Sound wide berth. And vice versa.

The anchor has been specially treated for the change of environment and is now in the care of the Tonquin Foundation.

Details: *Tonquin Foundation, Tofino: (250) 725-4488; http://www.tonquinfoundation.org/. On the Archives page is a 97-page report of the project; the Maritime Discovery Centre is at 566C Campbell St; call before visiting.*
An account of the massacre is in Washington Irving's Astoria (1835): http://www.xmission.com/~drudy/mtman/html/astoria/index.html.

80 Cougar Annie's Garden

In Clayoquot's many roadless reaches, Boat Basin, in the lee of Hesquiat Peninsula, is one of the remotest — 55 kilometres northwest of Tofino. Not the most likely place for a show garden — a 2-hectare plot hacked out of thick undergrowth amid forests of cedar, spruce and hemlock, ringed by mountain slopes.

Cougar Annie's Garden is the largest known pioneer garden on the island's west coast. Its many pathways provide glimpses of a once-flourishing homestead, the buildings slowly returning to nature.

The garden captures the spirit of those who settled in Clayoquot Sound — both early and late. Fact is, this is the garden's second go-round. Indeed, it is an epic tale of wilderness living that is still being told.

The Rae-Arthur family arrived in 1915, and Ada Annie started the ceaseless work of land clearing while raising eight children. Her husband Willie was not cut out for pioneering. He was more of a house-husband. The older children helped to pull stumps.

Cougar Annie became a well-known figure around Clayoquot Sound, with her four husbands — serially — and her mail-order seed and plant business, which evolved into the Boat Basin post office.

A well-spoken, cultured person, Ada Annie famously defended her turf with aggressive use of firearms. To make ends meet, she hunted cougar for bounty. A later acquaintance remembered "a tiny old lady with hands like a logger."

Ada Annie did manage to get a couple of husbands interested in gardening. She was an endearing character, with an energy that attracted others. In later years, her home became the retirement project of a Vancouver stockbroker.

Peter Buckland bought the place and allowed her to stay there into her 90s. He set to work maintaining and restoring the garden and orchard. He endowed the non-profit Boat Basin Foundation to keep Cougar Annie's Garden going and promote awareness of rainforest ecosystems.

If you go back to the beginning — with the help of Margaret Horsfield's substantial biography *Cougar Annie's Garden* — and look at the Vancouver wedding picture of Ada Annie Jordan and Willie Rae-Arthur, you can see great clarity in the eyes of the young woman. Someone recollected she had the eyes of a seer.

Maybe the garden came from that visionary state. After all, here it is, nearly a century later, flourishing again. As always, there are glitches. The latest is financial: the Foundation has put Cougar Annie's Garden up for sale.

Details: *Boat Basin Foundation: http://www.boatbasin.org/garden.htm.*
Opens Cougar Annie's Garden and the Temperate Rainforest Field Study Centre
to the public interested in "education, preservation and heritage" in season. Day-
trips are encouraged; accommodations are Spartan. "We welcome motivated,
independent people with a keen interest in the area. For your own safety, all visi-
tors should be reasonably physically fit."
Reading: Cougar Annie's Garden *by Margaret Horsfield (Salal Books, 2000).*

Northern Vancouver Island and adjacent Islands

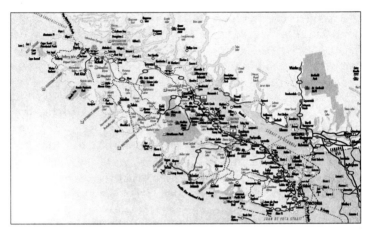

The northern reaches of Vancouver Island include the wonderfully scenic mountains in Strathcona Park, the island-strewn waters of the northeast coast, the deep channels and inlets of the west coast, and a tiny island off the northern tip where a million seabirds breed. The natural wonders of this remote region include fascinating congregations of orca whales in the Broughton Archipelago and the superlative forests of Nimpkish Island and White River. Campbell River, salmon fishing "capital of the world," is the gateway to a region with about 60,000 residents. Their numbers include two remarkable environmentalists, decades apart in time, pledged to protect our wild salmon.

81 Campbell River

Campbell River is the gateway to the north island. The post-industrial city of 38,000 (2007 est) sits by the southern entrance of Discovery Passage, just at the north end of Georgia Strait. The waterway is a funnel for traffic between Georgia Strait ports and the north island, north coast and north Pacific Ocean.

Campbell River is also a funnel for overland traffic. The daunting relief of the Beaufort Range squeezes roadways onto a narrow lowland strip. If you're bound to or from Strathcona Park or Nootka Sound on Highway 28 or the North Island on Highway 19, you'll go through Campbell River.

From the south the way to approach Campbell River is by way of the scenic Oceanside highway (19A). Route 19, the so-called Inland Highway, speeds motorists past the downtown.

On the southern fringe of downtown Campbell River is the historic district. There you will find the splendid Discovery Fishing Pier. The view across the 2-km passage is worth an excursion by itself. It's a good place to take in Campbell River's maritime life, armed perhaps with an ice cream cone from the take-out on the pier.

You'll spot fishing boats — nowadays mostly for sport rather than commerce — tugs with barges, whale- or bear-watching Zodiacs, pods of kayakers. The occasional freighter or container carrier from the north Pacific slides down the passage. You may see a multitude of Alaska-bound monster yachts and a few cruise ships.

Near the pier is the impressive Maritime Heritage Centre. It houses the fishing boat depicted on Canada's $5 dollar bill from 1972 to 1986. The seiner belonged to Harry Assu, late chief of the We Wai Kai First Nation of Cape Mudge on nearby Quadra Island.

For more than 100 years Campbell River has been celebrated as a salmon sportfishing centre with — as Assu put it in his readable memoir *Assu of Cape Mudge* — five species of Pacific Salmon readily available year-round. You'll almost always find some fishers trying their luck on the pier. You can rent the gear and buy a license on the spot.

A two-block stretch north of the centre is known as Historic Pier Street. This is where the original Campbell River steamship wharf stood, across the street from the Willows Hotel, the town's first building (1904). Loggers bound to and from remote logging camps put up there.

Informative markers throughout the downtown area recapitulate the heritage of this blue-collar town.

The excellent Museum at Campbell River is a short walk south of the Maritime Heritage Centre. Among its exhibits is the recreated Willows Hotel entrance and lobby. A theatre shows a short film about the local author and pioneer conservationist Roderick Haig-Brown.

The museum website has fascinating portfolios of historical photos. A Moment in Time features the work of the early 20th century photographer Henry Twidle of Quadra Island.

Campbell River is near the northern margin of the great Douglas fir forest. In 1906 the International Timber Company started railway logging 12,000 hectares of forestland between the Oyster and Campbell rivers. Trackage and a log dump occupied much of downtown Campbell River.

High-lead logging was the rule, and the workers were housed in camps. Their danger-filled work was captured in Haig-Brown's novel *Timber*. Campbell River was their Saturday-night party town.

An era that began with Campbell River's first sawmill (1922) came to a shocking end in 2010 when the nearby Duncan Bay pulp and paper complex, including the city's last sawmill, closed for good.

Surprisingly, in 2008-09, even after more than 700 mill workers were let go, the area's population increased modestly. It has a large and growing community of artists and crafters. Poised at nature's doorstep, Campbell River's attraction as a place to live includes relatively cheap property, while its fame as a salmon fishing centre is helping the town become a base for adventure recreation. Wildlife is the big draw — whales, sea lions and other marine mammals, bears of several kinds — viewed up-close from tour boats or kayaks.

From the pier, you barely get a glimpse of the region's fabulous wild-life habitat — the near-wilderness of the Discovery Islands, their intricate waterways and the dramatic fjord-carved mainland coast beyond.

Details: *Maritime Heritage Centre, 621 Island Highway, (250) 286-3161, http:// www.maritimeheritagecentre.ca/.*
Museum at Campbell River, 450 Island Highway, (250) 287-3103: http://www. crmuseum.ca/index.html.
Readings: Assu of Cape Mudge: Recollections of a Coastal Indian Chief *by Harry Assu (Vancouver: UBC Press, 1989).*
Timber: A Novel of Pacific Northwest Loggers *by Roderick Haig-Brown (1942, reprinted Oregon State University Press, 1993).*

82   Haig-Brown House

The Haig-Brown family are Vancouver Island royalty. Writer and naturalist Roderick Haig-Brown (1908-1976) put the island on the map with a stream of books about nature and conservation.

He wrote with direct knowledge and keen emotion about the many little rivers of the north island. He knew them well from having logged, guided, hunted and fished — especially fished — since first arriving here at age 19.

In 1934 the expat British adventurer married the intellectual Seattle-born Ann Elmore (1908-1990). By prenuptial agreement, Ann always typed up Rod's longhand drafts. They settled down on an 8-hectare farm beside the Campbell River, raised a family and created quite a legacy.

Haig-Brown House is now a riverfront bed-and-breakfast inn during summer months. It has an ambience that is at once literary, environmental and historical.

The Haig-Browns' charming gardens and shady riverfront, the fields and second-growth forest are intact, although reduced in size. The setting is so quiet you can hear the river through an open window.

A few who arrive at Haig-Brown House are on pilgrimage. They grew up reading *Starbuck Valley Winter* or *Saltwater Summer*, adventure books for young readers. Or *A River Never Sleeps* or *Measure of the Year* awakened their love of nature.

Some visitors are moved when they sit in the study and handle books in the author's library. The study and three bedrooms are substantially unchanged.

Occasionally, guests are on a sentimental journey. They found safe harbour here during a difficult time. Haig-Brown, a lay magistrate, was the Provincial Court judge for much of the north island and adjacent mainland coast. Over three decades he heard 200 to 300 cases a year, everything from DUI to petty theft to assault.

The shadow of hardship fell across many a misdemeanour. Rather than handing down sentences that made difficult situations worse, he often gave an offender some work and a place to stay.

Many who stayed at the Haig-Browns' were battered women. Ann Haig-Brown took a special interest in victims of domestic violence. Her care was recognized at the 1988 opening of the Ann Elmore Transition House.

Rod Haig-Brown published 25 books (some co-authored) in his lifetime. He built a durable reputation as an authority on fly fishing. Before Haig-Brown, few had written about fishing for steelhead, the feisty seagoing rainbow trout. Once there were native steelhead populations in 200 streams on Vancouver Island. To catch a 5-lb steelhead with a dry fly was the epitome of joy for Haig-Brown.

One of Canada's first conservationists, Haig-Brown bore witness to the destruction of countless little rivers and their runs of salmon and trout — directly, by clearcut logging and damming, and indirectly by pollution from mine tailings.

Articles poured out of his pen, drawing attention to the impoverishment of the commons by the industrial juggernaut. He equated the protection of Earth's productivity with our very survival and often gave vent to a deep pessimism. A philosophical mind was able to draw inclusiveness from this peril:

"It is in searching out the land, learning to live in it, learning to use it, that we have been shaped and tempered," he wrote in *Maclean's* magazine in 1973. "We have made many mistakes, some willful, some founded in ignorance, and we have not always shaped ourselves well.

"But I love the best of our intentions, hopes and desires, and I love the soul of Canada, the striving for unity and justice that exists in some degree in all of us."

Details: *Haig-Brown Heritage House, 2250 Campbell River Rd (Highway 28), Campbell River, (250) 286-6646; http://www.haig-brown.bc.ca/.*
Manager/host Sandra Chow's blog of visitors: http://haig-brownhouse.blogspot.com/.
Haig-Brown Kingfisher Creek Society restored the flow through the Haig-Brown property of a much-culverted salmon-bearing creek: http://www.haig-brown. bc.ca/kingfisher/about.html.
Reading: Deep Currents: Roderick and Ann Haig-Brown *by Valerie Haig-Brown (Victoria: Orca Books, 1997).*

83	**Elk Falls**

Thundering, elemental Elk Falls is just an 8-kilometre drive from Campbell River. (It's the city's *other* icon.) A network of delightful trails provides access to the 25-metre-high falls. There's a good hike in along the lower Campbell River.

Elk Falls Park was established in 1940 to protect more than 1,000 hectares of mostly second-growth forest around the magnificent falls. The ink was barely dry when the river was harnessed for hydroelectric power. The John Hart Dam, completed in 1947 just upriver from Elk Falls, shunts some

TAKE 5 GODFREY STEPHENS'
ANCHORAGES IN PARADISE

Bohemian world traveller, psychedelic artist and carver Godfrey Stephens has been a boatman in these waters since the 1960s. He's just putting the finishing touches to his latest creation, a 44-ft steel-hulled sailboat, Mungo ChingTing. "Mungo Martin was chief of the Kwakiutl, a great carver and mentor. ChingTing means 'dragon fly' in Chinese. With its red junk-rigged sails, that's what the boat looks like."

1. Sea Otter Cove, west of San Josef Bay; you can walk west over the headland to a wild windswept beach on Lowrie Bay.

2. Columbia Cove/Peddler's Cove on the South side of Brooks Peninsula; you walk southwest to an outside beach. Watch out for cougars!

3. The head of Mathilda Inlet, near Ahousaht, has warm springs, where Gordon Gibson, the Bull of the Woods, constructed a concrete tank. A trail south leads to Whitesand Beach, where there are vistas of Clayoquot Sound.

4. Sandy Island Marine Park is a very nice open area at the north end of Denman Island. Henry Bay, looking west toward Union Bay, provides shelter from winds.

5. God's Pocket is a group of islands on Queen Charlotte Strait. One of them has sheltered anchorage and a dock where I once sought refuge — a memorable place.

of the Campbell into 1.9-km-long wooden penstocks. They feed turbines at the John Hart Generating Station.

Getting to the falls requires some navigation through these industrial sites. There are parking lots and trailheads near both the dam and the generating station. A parking lot near the John Hart Dam is closest to the falls. The turnoff is 2.8 km W of the Quinsam River bridge on Highway 28. The road crosses the dam and bears right towards the parking lots.

Then there's a choice. For parking more convenient to the falls, follow the R fork. The trails are short and easy.

For more challenging trails, follow the L fork to the more northerly parking lot. The Elk Falls Trail winds along the river through a beautiful remnant old-growth forest of Douglas fir and western redcedar. There are lookouts near smaller waterfalls en route to a spectacular overview of Elk Falls and the sheer rock canyon below. The trail has steep sections and unprotected dropoffs.

For parking near the generating station, the turnoff is 0.75 km W of the Quinsam River bridge. The Canyon View Trail is a 4-km loop along the banks of the lower river. The western terminus is a footbridge near the generating station; its eastern terminus is a logging bridge 0.4 km E of the Quinsam River bridge.

Elk Falls poses an impassible barrier to migrating fish, and runs are confined to the 5-km lower Campbell. The Canyon View river walk has many points for observing runs of salmon and seagoing trout in season. You may spot some river kayakers as well as abundant wildlife.

The Canyon View Trail offers a way to approach Elk Falls on foot. Near the footbridge at the generating station is the eastern terminus of the 2.4-km Millennium Trail. This trail follows the impressive canyon upstream to link with the Elk Falls trails.

Details: *Elk Falls Provincial Park: http://www.env.gov.bc.ca/bcparks/explore/ parkpgs/elk_falls/. Has a 122-site campground on the Quinsam R.*
John Hart Dam: http://www.bchydro.com/community/recreation_areas/john_hart.html.

84 Quadra Island

A 10-minute ferry ride across Discovery Passage from Campbell River lands you in briny Quathiaski Cove on Quadra Island, population 2,700. The picturesque cove is a maritime service centre, with fishing boats bobbing at the docks. A cannery was once the local mainstay.

The largest of the Discovery Islands (area 27,600 hectares), Quadra is famous more and more for world-class pottery. There's a studio tour and arts festival every June. Quadra's more settled southern peninsula supports a number of smallhold farms — even a winery — and every

Saturday in season at the Quathiaski shopping centre, a farm market.

Southern Quadra is relatively flat and bike-friendly, at least compared with the gravel logging roads of the rugged north side. A number of interesting destinations are just a short hop from the ferry.

Rebecca Spit is a 2-km-long finger of sand enclosed in a 177-hectare day-use park that offers many trails through forest and field to outside beaches with engaging views eastward to Cortes Island.

A nice campground on nearby Drew Harbour is run by the We Wai Kai nation. It's surrounded by nature — but good luck getting a waterfront campsite after the beginning of the season. We have picked oysters off the outside beach and cooked them for dinner there. Otherwise, Heriot Bay has a store, and the venerable Heriot Bay Inn, a restaurant.

Tsa-Kwa-Luten Lodge has a gorgeous location at the opening of Discovery Passage. The First Nations-themed establishment sits on an eminence above an expanse of rocky beach, with various accommodations, including waterfront cottages with kitchenettes.

In the nearby We Wai Kai First Nation village of Yaculta (Cape Mudge) is the Nuyumabales Cultural Centre. The museum displays an important collection of Potlatch treasures and regalia confiscated by the government of Canada in the 1920s and returned from three museums in 1979.

Cape Mudge Lighthouse, near the lodge, is the islands' only manned lighthouse that is accessible by road and open to visitors. Built in 1898, it's staffed by the Canadian Coast Guard.

Details: *Quadra Island is accessible by BC Ferries with daily service from Campbell River and Cortes Island.*
Rebecca Spit Marine Provincial Park: http://www.env.gov.bc.ca/bcparks/explore/ parkpgs/rebecca/.
We Wai Kai campsite, Heriot Bay Rd, Quadra Id, (250) 285-3111; http://www. wwkcampsite.ca/.
Tsa-Kwa-Luten Lodge, 1 Lighthouse Rd, Quadra Id; 1-800-665-7745: http://www. capemudgeresort.bc.ca/.
Nuyumbalees Cultural Centre, 34 WeWay Road, Cape Mudge Village; (250) 285-3733; http://www.nuyumbalees.com/.
Quadra Island Artists, a directory: http://www.quadraislandarts.com/.

85 | Hollyhock

People flock to this rural retreat for refreshment and renewal. You get with your tribe at Hollyhock. The program of experiential five-day workshops are the draw.

Let's see — shall I do Taming the Hungry Ghost with Gabor Maté, MD? — Or Jan Zwicky's Poetry and Contemplation? — Or the Wild Peace

Family Retreat, combining "compassionate nonviolent communication with ancient wilderness awareness teachings?" — Or (my preference) all of the above?

Hollyhock's program runs mid-March to the end of October and is deep. The atmosphere gets pretty electric mid-summer, when it's in full swing. Over its 28 years Hollyhock has evolved from a focus mostly on personal development more to encouraging social change through the Business, Leadership and Social Change component of the program.

The surroundings are spectacular — south-facing waterfront that takes in a scenic archipelago, looks east into the heart of the Coast Mountains and south across the Strait of Georgia to the big island. I'm sure a lot of people come just to drink it all in.

Hollyhock's residential ambience is irresistible. There are little hideaway cabins in quiet meadows and upscale waterfront digs. You can go there on a retreat and just hang out — do the daily yoga, go for a guided nature walk, nosh on the outstanding vegetarian fare, go kayaking, get a massage. It's the end of the road.

The setting is lovely, with pathways, a 1-hectare garden, porches and lawns.

Ahem, the bill. For the quality of the experience, it's surprisingly reasonable. You're going to pay $1000-1800CDN per person for a five-day workshop, lodging and meals. Less, of course, for a holiday visit.

Transformative.

Details: *Hollyhock Educational Retreat Centre, Cortes Id: (800) 933-6339 or (250) 935-6576 (outside North America); www.hollyhock.ca. The website is worth a tour. Rex Weyler's account of how Hollyhock got its name gave me shivers. Good videos, too.*
Cortes Island is rural and isolated; it is two ferry trips from Campbell River, one from Powell River.

86 Strathcona Park Lodge

Strathcona Park Lodge is an outdoor adventure centre on Upper Campbell Lake. It introduces people to the wonders of wilderness travel — climbing the myriad of peaks in Strathcona Park, kayaking on the east or west coast, hiking on sea-lashed Nootka Island. The Lodge provides the equipment, the transport, the guides, and meals.

Its enthusiastic staff — many trained in the centre's outdoor leadership program — also train novices in wilderness travel, mostly in the benign surroundings of the Lodge, along the lakeshore and amid nearby rocky outcrops.

Guests stay in rustic cabins or suites and can either bring their own supplies or dine at the Lodge.

You can sign up for all-inclusive multi-day packages. You might learn how to exit an ocean kayak in shallow water in the morning … practice rapelling down a 10-m high bluff in the afternoon … join a guided nature walk around the bog in the evening.

It's less a lodge than a year-round camp. For families on a budget with young children, I'd say it's unbeatable.

The Lodge was the vision of Myrna and Jim Boulding. Their outdoor education program was based on a deep belief in the value of the wilderness experience. Their son Jamie Boulding and his partner Christine Clarke are now the co-directors. Both have won awards for outdoor education.

The Lodge is close to the alpine wonders of central Strathcona Park but not actually in the park.

It's less than an hour to either the west coast near Nootka Sound or Johnstone Strait to the east.

The setting is quite scenic — on a lake about 20 km long and 1.5 km wide, surrounded by low mountains, with dramatic views westward into the heart of the range. Pristine wilderness it is not — Upper Campbell Lake is the reservoir of the Strathcona Dam. The lake's much-enlarged shores are a study in altered landscapes.

Details: *Strathcona Park Lodge & Outdoor Education Centre, 41040 Gold River Rd (Highway 28), 42 km west of Campbell River, (250) 286-3122: http://www.strathcona.bc.ca. Also operates a chalet at Mt Washington ski resort.*

87 Strathcona Park at 100

Strathcona was BC's first provincial park, created in 1911 by an act of the BC Parliament to protect the alpine splendour of central Vancouver Island — its myriad vistas of jagged peaks … exquisite subalpine valleys dotted with turquoise lakes … the enchanting Buttle Lake. The framers were guided by a Banff-like vision of a mountain wilderness set aside for public enjoyment, with railway access and hotels. Extractive industries were excluded.

The centenary of Strathcona Park is cause for celebration. The park now protects a total of 245,807 hectares. There have been significant additions — like the intact pristine Megin-Talbot watershed in Clayoquot Sound, added to the park in 1995. Its 27,390 hectares comprise the largest remaining undisturbed watershed on the island. Three core areas totaling 122,500 hectares have extra protection as wilderness conservancies.

Do parks really protect land? Valid question — in the case of Strathcona, the reality doesn't come close to matching the rhetoric.

From the get-go, the Strathcona Park Act was amended (1913) to allow damming of water. Another amendment in 1918 allowed mineral exploration. Claims were being staked anyway.

After World War II, hydroelectric dams brought development into the park. The Campbell River drains Buttle, Upper and Lower Campbell lakes. Soon the rich bottomland around the Campbell lakes became reservoirs. In 1952 the hydro authority proposed building the Strathcona Dam and raising the water level of Buttle Lake. Edged with ancient forests, Buttle was called the most beautiful lake in the province. Because part of the lake is in Strathcona Park, there were public hearings. Roderick Haig-Brown waged a one-man campaign against the project. The dam went ahead, with its height reduced, and Buttle became a reservoir, its shoreline rising and dropping seasonally with the demand for electricity.

Meanwhile, the boundaries of the park have been much altered. Strathcona has been used as a land bank to acquire parkland elsewhere. It started with Pacific Rim National Park. Logging companies were given bits around the edges of Strathcona Park to compensate for timber rights cancelled when Pacific Rim Park was created. These land swaps were back-room deals.

The last straw came in 1988. A government-backed proposal would have drained beautiful Cream Lake and created a second mine in the park (the Westmin Mine has operated there since the 1960s). Local citizens formed the Friends of Strathcona Park. They staged a peaceful blockade that saw 64 law-abiding people arrested.

The BC government changed its tune, and a master plan has been in place since 1993. The master plan allows only minimal human impacts in Strathcona. A public advisory group was set up to review park-use proposals. Sadly, the chiseling continues.

The government, meanwhile, cries poor, and amenities in the park are in sorry repair — trails unmaintained, bridges down. Several trails have been closed for safety reasons, to the exclusion of the hiking public. How's that for irony?

Friends of Strathcona Park has recently launched Take Back the Park, a volunteer trail-rebuilding project. (To the government's credit — or thanks to pressure exerted by the Friends — BC Parks budgeted $330,000 to replace two bridges and repair a section of boardwalk in 2010.) For those who love the park and know it best, Strathcona's centennial is bittersweet.

Details: *Strathcona Provincial Park: http://www.env.gov.bc.ca/bcparks/explore/parkpgs/strath/. Travel advisories posted regularly.*

Vehicle access to Strathcona Park is via the Buttle Lake road, off Highway 28 W of Campbell River. It skirts the east side of the lake (22 km long and barely 1 km across), with campgrounds and day-use areas along the way. Trailheads to Forbidden Plateau are on the east, and Marble Meadows on the west. There's often heavy vehicle traffic on the road to and from the Westmin mine.

Beyond Nootka, a compilation of mountaineering stories by Lindsay Elms: http://members.shaw.ca/beyondnootka/

Friends of Strathcona Park: http://friendsofstrathcona.org/. Regular postings of

reliable news about the realities of protection.
Strathcona Provincial Park 1911-2011: http://ekoscommunications.com/node/754.
The plundering of Strathcona Park as recounted by retired BC Parks staff.

88   The Golden Hinde

The heart of Vancouver Island is a cluster of craggy peaks surrounded by ramparts of granite. In the middle of this grandeur stands The Golden Hinde, the island's highest point, 2,200 metres above sea level.

The first known ascent was in 1914. The Hinde was conquered by yours truly in 1988. It's not that difficult — there is a bit of scrambling, but no rock climbing. The reward for my ascent was a windy overview of the entire central island from one very pointed peak.

The view takes in most of Strathcona Park. One of Strathcona's three nature conservancies encloses the area west of Buttle Lake. No motorized vehicles are allowed and no fly-ins. There aren't even trails, just the occasional stone marker. No fires are allowed, although campers can bring gas stoves.

Considering the rugged terrain, central Strathcona is remarkably accessible. The trick is to travel on the granite ridges. Several interconnected hiking routes cross the park at middle elevations. Getting up and down can be challenging.

A hiking expedition to Golden Hinde could be completed in three long days — a day from the Myra Falls mine to Burman Lake, a day for the ascent and a day to return. If you have arranged to hike across the area and be picked up, allow three days to hike through the Elk River Valley to or from Burman Lake.

It's wise to allow an extra day for the unexpected. North of Burman Lake we found ourselves in deep snow — in September. We came to the edge of the granite ridge. A thick whiteout prevented us from seeing into the valley that was our destination. Did I mention there are no trails? Hypothermia reared its ugly head.

Luckily, a party of rangers materialized, heading out on their last hike of the season. One of them stood on the edge of the ridge and was able, by hearing alone, to distinguish two creeks flowing in opposite directions far below. We found our route down by aiming between the two.

Further north, a procession of impossibly scenic alpine vistas unfolds — cloud-capped mountains above, jewel-like lakes in sculpted valleys below. Approaching Elk River Pass you skirt the dramatically stark Landslide Lake.

Travel in that elevated country requires psychological preparation, self-sufficiency and orienting skills. A good map, guidebook and compass are essential. Hazards are many — one of our party slipped on wet heather covering a boulder and just about required a medevac. (Best plan is to travel in parties of four.)

It's all worth it for the exhilaration of getting above treeline at the very centre of the island.

Details: *Guidebook: Hiking Trails 3: Northern Vancouver Island, 10th edition, 2008. Has good maps.*
Traiheads: On the east, from the BC Parks parking lot just past the Myra Falls mine, up the Philips Ridge Trail. On the north, from Highway 28 up the Elk River trail. There's also a route (water access only) from Buttle Lake up the Marble Meadows trail.

89 Gold River Caves

Gold River is one tenacious west coast community. It ranges up a long hill, a well-serviced suburb of ranchers on spacious view lots. Gold River was a planned community, built in the 1960s to house the families of loggers and workers in the pulp mill on nearby Muchalat Inlet. The village, 90 kilometres west of Campbell River on Highway 28, is an isolated centre in a sea of mountains. But it was rich in amenities and services. It had an aquatic centre, an arena, a golf course, parks and baseball diamonds.

A newsprint mill was added in the 1980s but soon shut down, followed by the troubled pulp mill in 1999. Four-fifth of Gold River's tax base vanioshed. Its population fell from an historic high of 2,225 (1981) to 1,359 (2001). The village's budget shrank to bare-bones maintenance. It has a since registered gains in residents. Many locals are hanging on, looking for better days.

Gold River's renown as a sport fishing centre generates modest revenues seasonally. It's also a service centre for Nootka Sound and the base of the passenger freighter MV *Uchuck III*. The town is a staging centre for recreation in Nootka Sound and Strathcona Park. Gold River's search for green economic growth includes a scheme that would use the pulp mill plant to generate power by burning garbage.

Another asset is the amazing number of caves that occur in the vicinity. Gold River calls itself itself the Caving Capital of Canada.

About four percent of Vancouver Island is covered in limestone formations known as karst. Rain water forms the weak solvent carbonic acid as it falls and percolates through the soils. Where karst occurs near the surface, the acid works on the limestone, dissolving the rock and establishing underground drainages. Where, on the other hand, a stream finds a sink point and flows through karst, it dissolves the limestone and forms caves.

When you look east from Gold River, you see the white of limestone. That's the surface karst of White Ridge, whose summit the average hiker can reach from Highway 28 in five arduous hours. White Ridge is protected in a 1,343-ha provincial park.

The deepest known cave on the island (and fourth deepest in Canada) is the 416-metre-deep Thanksgiving Cave. The longest known caves on the island (Canada's fourth longest) is the Weymer Creek system with more than 13 kilometres of mapped passages. Both are near Gold River in rough backcountry — don't even think of going there unless you're an experienced, well-prepared caver.

Much more accessible to casual visitors are the Upana Caves, a system more than 500 metres long with 15 entrances, 17 kilometres west of Gold River. The Upana River flows in and out of the caves, and there are some openings where it flows over karst and forms waterfalls. A self-guided tour, for which there is a map, takes less than an hour.

Details: *Village of Gold River: http://www.goldriver.ca/explore/gold-river-caving-rockclimbing.php.*
Information about the Upana Caves: (250) 283-7334.
Vancouver Island Cave Exploration Group: http://www.cancaver.ca/bc/viceg/.
Weymer Creek Provincial Park: http://www.env.gov.bc.ca/bcparks/explore/park-pgs/weymr_cr/.
White Ridge Provincial Park: http://www.env.gov.bc.ca/bcparks/explore/parkpgs/wht_ridg/.
Energy from Waste in Gold River, made locally to show support: http://www.you-tube.com/watch?v=O4P74Uv5E60.

90 Yuquot

The tiny outpost of Yuquot (Friendly Cove) on Nootka Island is the site of an ancient First Nations whaling base and summer village. It's also the place of Europeans' first landing on the Northwest Coast — Captain James Cook, HMS *Resolution* and *Discovery*, 1778.

The passenger freighter MV *Uchuck III* calls in at Yuquot. During the summer, you can make the scenic 40-km Saturday trip from Gold River, get a terrific welcome from the Mowchaht/Muchalaht First Nation, stroll around, and return the same day.

A wooden helicopter pad near the lighthouse provides lofty views of Yuquot's inner and outer bays. We were there early in September, and our attention was drawn to the rocky point in between. About 100 metres away, a humpback whale was diving, tossing its giant flukes. Whales rub, we were told, on the gravel beaches.

Deeper immersion in West Coast wilderness and culture is recommended. You can go out on Saturday and stay a few nights in a beachfront rustic cabin at Yuquot; you bring your own bedding, lighting and food. The Mowachaht/Muchalaht First Nation also runs a campground. *Uchuck III* will call back during its regular 2-day circuit of Nootka and

Kyuquot sounds, servicing logging camps, fish farms, Tahsis, Zeballos, Esperanza and other isolated communities. You can also get dropped off or picked up by chartering a water taxi or float plane in Gold River.

A bolder approach is to load your kayak aboard the *Uchuck* and be put in the water in your craft. Some are bound for the wilderness reaches of Santa Gertrudis-Boca del Infierno Park (435 hectares) and Bligh Island Marine Park (4,455 hectares). Advanced skills are required for Nootka Sound's fast waters, considerable swell and strong westerly winds. (*Yuquot* means *where winds blow from every direction*.)

Or take a backpack and hike the rough 35-km trail across the outer coast of Nootka Island. Beautiful! There are crossings — be sure to take tide tables.

Europeans called the old village *Nootka*. It became a base of exploration, the centre of a flourishing fur trade and the site of several brief settlements. On the maps of the day, Nootka was the only place between Spanish California and Russian Alaska.

From the contact emerged a picture of First Nations society unrivalled for human interest. A wealth of eyewitness reports was published by journal-keepers on visiting vessels. The most famous of these is likely *The Adventures and Suffering of John Jewitt*.

A native of England, Jewitt shipped aboard the American trader *Boston* as an armourer at age 19. Americans had gained control of the sea otter trade. Yankee entrepreneurs carried the highly-prized pelts between First Nations suppliers and the Chinese market. They plied this coast until, within a few decades, the animal was extirpated.

The *Boston* arrived in Nootka Sound in March 1803 and traded with the Mowachaht chief Maquinna. Friendly relations led to the gift of a rifle to the chief — followed by harsh words over what Maquinna called a *peshak* (bad) lock on the rifle. The captain "called the king a liar, adding other opprobrious terms, and taking the gun from him, tossed it indignantly into the cabin, and calling me to him, said, 'John, this fellow has broken this beautiful fowling-piece, see if you can mend it.'"

Jewitt, a blacksmith, and the ship's sailmaker were the only ones spared in the massacre that revenged the insult. It was not the worst Maquinna had suffered at the hands of lowlife shipmen, by far. Four of his chiefs had been assassinated by Captain Martinez and "upwards of 20" men killed by Captain Hanna, including several chiefs. Maquinna was lucky to have escaped with his life.

The two were enslaved. Jewitt spent the better part of three years in Nootka Sound. His journal was an unused accounts book from the ship. Jewitt made ink "by boiling the juice of the blackberry with a mixture of finely powdered charcoal, and filtering it through a cloth."

Yuquot was a village of 20 houses. The biggest, chief Maquinna's, measured 45 metres by 12 metres. Every September, the entire village was dismantled, except for the massive log house-frames, "to pass the autumn and winter at Tashees and Cooptee." Tashees (Tahsis), the winter village, lay "about thirty miles up the Sound, in a deep bay."

The cedar-plank walls and roofs were removed from the houses and carried away. "To an European, such a removal exhibits a scene quite novel and strange: canoes piled up with boards and boxes, and filled with men, women, and children, of all ranks and sizes, making the air resound with their cries and songs."

Maquinna and his family opened their hearts to Jewitt. The Englishman was a favourite of Maquinna's, especially after making the chief a steel whaling harpoon. The way the family drew him into their confidences is deeply moving. Love is not too strong a word. Jewitt maintained a steely reserve.

Jewitt's narrative captures the intimate details of Nuu-Chah-Nulth life. The ranking men, for example, while fearsome warriors and fearless whalers, spent hours painting their faces. They applied sparkles and powdered their hair with white down. The women did not share the men's taste for make-up.

The captives escaped to the first American ship that called in after the massacre. Jewitt's devilish ruse is one for the movies. He managed to retrieve the *Boston's* plundered goods as well — all without loss of life or face.

Little remains of old Yuquot. Enduring buildings include a lighthouse (built 1911) and a cultural centre in a former church (built 1956).

Details: *Uchuck III, Nootka Sound Service, end of Highway 28, Gold River: 1-877-824-8253 or (250) 283-2515; http://www.mvuchuck.com/. The weekly summer schedule changes from time to time.*
Mowachaht/Muchalaht First Nation: http://www.yuquot.ca/yuquot.html.
Accommodations at Yuquot: (250) 850-5239. Ask for Cabin 6, facing the outside coast.
Reading: The Adventures and Suffering of John R. Jewitt, 1824 Scottish edition in Open Library: http://openlibrary.org/books/OL7227807M/adventures_and_sufferings_of_John_R._Jewitt.

91 Kyuquot/Brooks

I can think of no more beautiful place than Spring Island. It's just off the northwest coast, between Kyuquot Sound (pronounced *kye YOO ct*) and the Brooks Peninsula. Less than 2 km across, Spring Id is dramatically varied — its leeward side is a broad bay that empties at low tide, revealing a profusion of sea life, while the windward side is a surfwashed prow of rock facing the open Pacific.

The scenic backdrop, about 25 kilometres west, is mountainous Brooks Peninsula. During the last glaciation, the Brooks was a rare ice-free area. It is a refugium of plant communities found nowhere else in North America. There are beautiful sand beaches on Brooks' eastern edge. The rest is inaccessible to all but the hardiest. Cape Cook is the roughest passage on the island.

A pristine wilderness area of some 52,000 hectares is protected in Muquin/Brooks Peninsula Provincial Park. It includes the Nasparti River, an intact drainage of old growth forest and abundant wildlife.

The nearby protected Bunsby Group of islands is a kayaker's paradise.

A major attraction for sea-based wildlife viewing is the core habitat of the sea otter, protected in the 35,000-hectare foreshore Checleset Bay Ecological Reserve. The once-vanished sea otter was reintroduced in 1969 with breeding pairs from Alaska. They have flourished, and their huge appetite for shellfish has generated biologically-rich kelp forests. (Some First Nations people view the sea otter as a competitor and take a dim view of their protected status.)

In an intact drainage in Kyuquot Sound, a mosaic of ecosytems is protected in Tahsish-Kwois Provincial Park (10,092 ha) and 70-ha Tahsish River Ecological Reserve. The valley's estuary and old-growth forest are prime habitat of the rare and endangered Roosevelt elk.

A grassy meadow on the north side of Spring Island furnishes the base camp of West Coast Expeditions, a kayak tour operation with an interesting history. Rupert Wong's family fled China during the Revolution and settled in Vancouver. His uncle, a commercial fisherman, discovered Spring Island. It evolved into a summer camp for the extended family. Rupert grew up navigating these waters and, after earning a degree in marine biology, started the kayaking outfit. It's now run by long-time associate Dave Pinel.

The open ocean with its long swells takes some getting used to. It's no place to trifle with nature. Expeditions, mostly by kayak but also in a V-bottom aluminum boat, touch many memorable places.

Details: *Kyuquot/Checleseht First Nation: http://www.kyuquot.ca/. Should be consulted before traveling in traditional territories.*

West Coast Expeditions: http://www.westcoastexpeditions.com/.

Muquin/Brooks Peninsula Provincial Park: http://www.env.gov.bc.ca/bcparks/ explore/parkpgs/brooks_peninsula/.

Big Bunsby Marine Provincial Park: http://www.env.gov.bc.ca/bcparks/explore/ parkpgs/big_bunsby/.

Checleset Bay Ecological Reserve: http://www.env.gov.bc.ca/bcparks/eco_reserve/ checleset_er.html. Non-consumptive recreational use only; permit required to land within the reserve.

Tahsish-Kwois Provincial Park: http://www.env.gov.bc.ca/bcparks/explore/park- pgs/tahsish/.

Tahsish River Ecological Reserve: http://www.env.gov.bc.ca/bcparks/eco_reserve/ tahsish_er.html.

92 White River Park

An old-growth Douglas fir forest of a grandeur comparable to Cathedral Grove stands beside a logging road south of the village of Sayward. Protected in 68-hectare White River Park, this amazing place is easily accessible. Just as amazing is the story of the loggers who put down their saws to save it.

In 1990 Don Zapp and Dave Luoma were falling trees in the White River valley. (A third faller, Dave Morrison, was on light duty.) They lived in Sayward and had worked for MacMillan Bloedel Ltd for 22 and 13 years respectively.

They came to a stand of giant Douglas firs and other conifers they knew to be the last old-growth in the valley. These were trees more than 85 metres in height — still vigorous, with intact tops. Luoma estimates the biggest of the Douglas firs to be 500 or 600 years old, some possibly 800 years old.

The three conferred and decided they just couldn't take down the magnificent trees. They faced possible dismissal and loss of seniority. Morrison, union chair at MB's Kelsey Bay Division, took it on. Fortunately, the company got onside, and in 1995 the provincial government protected the ancient forest.

Ready for our close-up, Mr DeMille — In 1994, the White River forest attracted the attention of a US film company. A softcore gothic romance, *The Scarlet Letter*, was shot there. Vancouver Island old-growth stood in for the vanished hardwood forest of 17th-century Massachusetts. The crew and cast — Demi Moore, Gary Oldman, Robert Duvall — stayed in Campbell River and choppered in to the site. Their legacy is a nice boardwalk through the park. The film? The *New York Times* called it "trashy and nonsensical."

Details: *White River Provincial Park is 25 km south of Highway 19 on the White River Main, a gravel logging road. From Highway 19, turn S on Hern Rd and at once take the R branch onto Oyer Rd; at 0.6 km take the L branch onto Salmon River Rd; at 1.0 km take the R fork onto the White River Main.*
Sayward is 73 km west of Campbell River on Highway 19.
BC Parks' page: http://www.env.gov.bc.ca/bcparks/explore/parkpgs/wht_river/.

93 Nimpkish Island

One of the most impressive forests of Douglas fir trees remaining in Canada grows on an 18-hectare alluvial flat in the upper Nimpkish River.

The huge Douglas firs, so tall relative to their girth, with deeply-indented bark, are clustered amid a younger forest of mostly western redcedar. The average height of the firs is 66 metres and their average diameter

1.3 m. The majority are believed to be 350-400 years old. It's easy to distinguish a number of bigger trees. The biggest rises 94 m and the widest measures 2.4 m in diameter. Those trees are believed older than 600 years.

One of the functions of ecological reserves is to protect remarkable places. The Nimpkish Island forest is considered taller overall than Cathedral Grove, although not as old. Compared to MacMillan Park it's tiny and out of the way. When the object is to preserve a superlative, though, isolation is a plus.

Nimpkish Island was part of the Canadian Forest Products (CanFor) Tree Farm Licence 37. Founder Leopold Bentley intended it to be a gift to his adoptive province. (The Bentley family emigrated from Austria in 1938.) Never happened. Under his successor, Peter Bentley, CanFor changed its tune. Nimpkish Island was held ransom. The BC Government coughed up nearly $1 million to compensate the company for lost timber rights.

We expect our protected areas to remain safe forevermore. Nimpkish Island furnishes an object lesson. As surrounding valleys have been logged, much severe flooding has ensued. There are huge gravel deposits around the island.

I've been on three trips to Nimpkish Island. It seems that, when the river becomes a torrent, it erodes the banks and all too often the roots of the giant firs. Winter storms bring them down. Riprap embankments have been installed as bulwarks against erosion, but the riverrine ecosystem is so dynamic there's no telling how Canada's tallest firs will fare.

Details: *Nimpkish Island Ecological Reserve is 18 km SE of Woss Camp on logging roads; it's accessible only by permit from BC Parks: http://www.env.gov.bc.ca/bcparks/eco_reserve/nimpkish_er.html.*

94 Broughton Archipelago

Broughton Archipelago is a magnificent near-wilderness in the remote tidal reaches between northeast Vancouver Island and the mainland coast, the renowned and much-visited habitat of orca whales and other sea mammals.

The archipelago comprises dozens of islands (the largest is Gilford, 38,200 hectares) and hundreds of islets and rocks that form the eastern boundary of Queen Charlotte Strait and straddle Knight Inlet. Johnstone and Broughton straits form its southern boundary. To north and east it becomes a maze of channels, islands and mainland peninsulas.

If you're headed for Malcolm or Cormorant islands, there is regular vehicle ferry service from Port McNeill to Sointula (population about 800) and Alert Bay (about 550).

Otherwise, you can hire a water taxi or float plane or tour with a group.

If your craft is self-propelled, you will note that Broughton has some of the scariest tidal currents anywhere. At some entrances there are maelstroms that eat craft both small and large, while other spots develop huge standing waves known as *haystacks* that can really throw a boat around.

The tiny community of Echo Bay on Gilford Island is en route to some of Broughton's remoter culs de sac. Nearby shores harbour the welcome Paddlers' Inn, with its two secluded cabins, one of them floating. Longtime resident Bill Proctor has a small museum crammed with artifacts from the watery work and lifestyle of yore. Broughton was for a while a lively centre of handlogging, where gyppos with steam donkeys on floating A-frames would tug a single log to the nearest mill. Rowboat fishers harvested waters that teemed with salmon and took them to floating canneries.

Broughton Archipelago Marine Park is a paradise of charming beaches and fascinating rock formations near Queen Charlotte Strait. The 11,679-hectare protected area (including land and water) is worth days of exploration. A circuit from Telegraph Cove totals about 90 kilometres.

The traditional territory of Kwakwaka'wakw-speaking nations, Broughton has an ancient history of settlement and use. There are shell middens everywhere and a wealth of petroglyphs and pictographs on rocks near sea level. On Village Island is an abandoned village with a musical name, Mamalilaculla.

Details: *Broughton Archipelago Marine Provincial Park: http://www.env.gov. bc.ca/bcparks/explore/parkpgs/broughton/.*
Paddlers' Inn, Simoon Sound, messages: (250) 230-0088; http://www.paddlersinn. ca/index.htm. Catered meals by arrangement.
Reading: Heart of the Raincoast: A Life Story *by Alexandra Morton and Billy Proctor (Horsdal & Schubart, 1998).*

95 Orcas

The most reliable place to see orcas — the whale formerly known as *killer*, AKA *blackfish* — is in the Broughton Archipelago. It's frequented by both resident pods — fish-eaters — and those of the larger transient orca, who roam the high seas and eat sea mammals. The archipelago is considered one of the finest orca habitats anywhere.

When our family went whale-watching in Broughton, we watched four pods meet in the open water — including a pod of transients — and enjoyed a talk on the matriarchy of orca pods.

Orca males are larger than females — they can weigh up to 10 tonnes — have more prominent dorsal fins, are more aggressive and thus more visible to human observers — yet studies of pod behaviour yielded the conclusion that they are typically led by the eldest female.

The presenter was a doctoral candidate at the University of California. She left her perch on a rock in the strait to talk to the group and returned there after the talk.

Also in the vicinity is the unique orca rubbing beach at Robson Bight near the mouth of the Tsitika River, protected since 1982 in Robson Bight (Michael Bigg) Ecological Reserve. The name memorializes a pioneering Canadian orca researcher.

Whale research is ongoing in Broughton. OrcaLab has been the Hanson Island facility of Paul Spong, a student of orca vocalization, since 1970. Spong is an outspoken advocate of the release of captive whales.

Whale-watching tour operators are based in Port McNeill, Port Hardy, Alert Bay, Sointula, Alder Bay and Telegraph Cove. Most offer wildlife-watching tours as well — to view, for example, grizzly bears foraging on mainland beaches.

It's worth checking tour operators' MO before signing up. Do they operate their craft non-intrusively? High-speed tour boats can stampede sea lion and seal colonies. Do they respect the 100-metre legal limit of approach to whales? Some venture closer and — with the best educational intentions — harass and even endanger the animals.

BC's pioneer whale-watching outfit is based in Telegraph Cove. Jim Borrowman moved to Telegraph Cove in the 1970s to work in the sawmill. When the owner retired, Jim bought the 17-metre-long diesel tug *Gikumi*. It was built in 1954 to tug logs to the mill. Soon its ample deck was carrying whale-watchers.

When Jim and Mary Borrowman started Stubbs Island Whale Watching in 1980, orcas were still being shot by fishermen. Their dwindling populations made a remarkable transition to beloved and protected species to veritable icon of nature.

Protection of orcas was hastened by the urging of people who had seen the magnificent mammals in the wild. (The northern resident population, numbering about 200, is listed as threatened under Canada's *Species at Risk Act.*)

Telegraph Cove is worth a visit to experience one of the island's treasures, a tiny former fishing village clinging to the rocky shore with a planked road over the water. The highly scenic boardwalk and adjacent buildings — cabins dating from the 1920s — have been converted to rustic lodgings (seasonal). Development of the opposite shore, has, unfortunately, compromised the isolated character of the cove.

Details: *Telegraph Cove is 202 km north of Campbell River, via Highway 19 and Beaver Cove Rd; follow the signs in; a little logging road travel at the end.*
Stubbs Island Whale Watching, reservations 1-800-665-3066; http://www.stubbs-island.com/.
Telegraph Cove Resort: http://www.telegraphcoveresort.com/lodging.html.
Robson Bight (Michael Bigg) Ecological Reserve: http://www.env.gov.bc.ca/

bcparks/eco_reserve/robsonb_er.html. Access is restricted.
OrcaLab: http://www.orcalab.org/. With an informative blog of observations and encounters in Broughton Archipelago.

96	Wild Salmon

The Icon of the Islands — the thing that best represents Vancouver Island's many parts and symbolizes the totality — is wild Pacific salmon.

One of the great wonders of nature is the migration of salmon from the freshwater streams of their birth to the ocean and then, after years in the sea, their return to the same stream to spawn and die.

In every corner of every island, along thousand of kilometres of coast and far inland, in every little creek and in the mighty rivers, the dance of red and silver life has gone on since time immemorial.

Each population of the six oceangoing species of salmon — and there are thousands — has adapted to a particular ecosystem. They return to the home range to perpetuate their genetic imprint. That's amazing.

They also leave their carcasses. Every spawned-out salmon carcass contributes nutrients to the forest that cradles every little creek and to the wildlife populations — bear, wolf, cougar — that use it.

All that rich biomass, so far in the forest — amazing.

Salmon have given us much besides.

Salmon was the staple of the traditional economies of First Nations on the coast and in the interior. Many richly expressive cultures were based on the abundance of fish.

Fishing was, after mining, coastal BC's foundational industry. Our society is to a degree based on the prosperity generated by the commercial salmon fishery and a host of canneries.

The commercial fishing boat, along with the axe, the rifle and the trap, supported the resourceful, independent lifestyle of generations of families on these islands.

It is now possible to see the end of that priceless legacy. We have taken the abundance of salmon for granted. We have abused the habitat. The runs are disappearing. The lights are going out.

One person who refuses to accept that fate is Alexandra Morton.

A marine biologist, Morton moved to the Broughton Archipelago to study whales. After her husband died in an underwater accident in 1984, Alexandra raised their two children there. Until recently the family lived in Echo Bay.

After 1987, when fish farms started to appear in Broughton's many inlets and channels — most owned by giant Norwegian companies — Morton started noting declines in salmon runs and suspected impairment of fry by sea lice from neighbouring open pens.

Sea lice are tiny leech-like critters that thrive in fish farms. Clouds of them have been observed to spread from the open pens, which are numerous in Broughton.

Sea lice attach themselves to salmon fry that are just emerging from the river environment and beginning to swim toward the ocean.

All it takes is one lousy louse to kill a fry.

A diligent biologist, Morton attracted collaborators who studied the link and published the findings in *Science* and other reputable journals. She became a dutiful reporter of changes in the local ecosystem of her beloved Broughton Archipelago.

Her work opened a Pandora's box of ridicule and denial. But the research has been amply borne out by science and experience in other places. Fish-farm sea lice are killing salmon by the millions before they ever reach the ocean. Unfortunately, that's only one ingredient of the deleterious soup that slops out of the fish farms and into the surrounding waters. The chemical treatment applied to control sea lice in the pens is highly toxic.

Wherever fish farms are set up in the paths of migrating salmon, the runs have declined. No fish farms — no declines. Morton urges a ban on pens open to the ocean. The fish farms need to be in tanks. The looming catastrophe is preventable to a degree.

Fish farms have operated largely without regulation in BC, thanks to a protocol that gave the Province the responsibility for protecting the ambient waters. The federal Department of Fisheries and Oceans has the constitutional responsibility to protect wild salmon habitat. In 2009 Morton went to court to compel the Department of Fisheries and Oceans to discharge its responsibility. She won.

In 2010 Morton organized a march from Campbell River to Victoria to protest the preventable decline of the islands' wild salmon. A crowd of 4,000-5,000 showed up at the steps of the Legislature in support. It was likely the largest environmental protest rally ever staged there.

At the rally Alexandra Morton was called a Canadian hero. There were effusions of love. Why? She has stirred the conscience of the polis. She leads by example, making use of one precious legacy — the democratic right of free speech and protest — to try to protect another.

Because, as e e cummings put it, *A world of made is not a world of born.*

Details: *Alexandra Morton's blog: http://alexandramorton.typepad.com/.*
Raincoast Research Society: http://www.raincoastresearch.org/about.htm.
Reading: A Stain Upon the Sea: West Coast Salmon Farming *by Stephen Hume, Alexandra Morton, et al (Madeira Park, BC: Harbour Publishing, 2004).*

97 Alert Bay

Alert Bay is the principal village of the Namgis First Nation, a Kwakwaka'wakw people of Broughton Strait. The famous village on Cormorant Island was often photographed when the bay was lined with wooden big houses, their facades painted and monumental poles carved and painted to display the owners' family crests.

None of that remains. Since 1980 the U'mista Cultural Centre has been a feature on the Alert Bay waterfront. The handsome museum displays goods confiscated by the government of Canada at a 1921 potlatch and restored to the First Nation latterly. The website has in-depth readings about the so-called Potlatch Collection.

Alert Bay is a vivid experience — an in-your-face place.

Once when up-island I dropped in on Will Malloff via the 10-kilometre ferry trip from Port McNeill to Alert Bay. Will invited me to stay and offered to show me around. A master craftsman and artist in wood, he led me to a carving room in a back corner of the former St Michael's residential school, where an older man sat and talked with a couple of young people. It was Saturday evening; more young people came and went.

The talk was light-hearted, but Will had to work to get a conversation going. I might as well have been a piece of furniture. One man was working on a bright yellow mask, made of a bulging semi-sphere of wood — it was perhaps a burl — on which he was painting a stylized face that was startlingly vivid.

I produced some of my books. The older man, whose name was Doug Cranmer, zeroed in on a picture in *Victoria a History in Photographs*. It was entitled *Cheslakee's village on Johnstone's Strait*, an 18th century engraving from a sketch of the nation's principal village at the mouth of the Nimpkish River. The print was published in *A Voyage of Discovery to the North Pacific Ocean and Round the World 1791-1795* by George Vancouver.

Cranmer pointed to the caption and asked, rhetorically, whether we were really on Johnstone Strait. It was a bit of a booby trap — Capt Vancouver himself named the local waters Broughton Strait after his second in command. The famous mariner died before the book was published. If the publisher didn't correct the error, I didn't feel the need to. I'm a bit sensitive on points of geography.

Another scolding followed. Cranmer found a photo of Alert Bay in *Wish You Were Here* to which I had appended the note, "The village of Alert Bay traces its beginnings only to about 1870, when two settlers from the Nimpkish River established a salmon saltery."

This started a discussion about the origins of Alert Bay, which I of course took personally. The point was, What did I know about their history and how did I know it? I defended my sources, the best ethnographic and historical and all that. Consensus emerged that there may have been a fish camp on Cormorant Island, but no village. Could have saved my breath.

Doug Cranmer (1927-2006) was a prominent carver and painter of the Namgis First Nation, known the world over for his mastery of both traditional and contemporary idioms. Now I think about it, his criticism was a gift. He pulled a pointer out of my writing that was valid for any subject. It was telling me to get closer.

Details: *Port McNeill-Alert Bay ferry: bcferries.com.*
Namgis First Nation land claim: http://www.firstnations.de/fisheries/kwakwak-awakw-namgis.htm.
U'mista Cultural Centre, Alert Bay: umista.ca.
Doug Cranmer: Whittling for a Living, by Eden Robinson (1994): http://www.moa.ubc.ca/Exhibitions/Online/Sourcebooks/Doug/page2.html.

98 The Suquash Mine Fiasco

On the island's wet and windy northeast coast, Highway 19 winds through the Suquash Basin, past the little-known Suquash mine, site of the botched beginning of the colony of Vancouver Island.

In 1836, the Hudson's Bay Company's paddle steamer *Beaver* called in at Suquash during its first year on the west coast. Coal had been reported there by a First Nations informant, and shortly HBC started buying coal from the Kwakiutl First Nation.

Steam-powered navy vessels began to visit in 1846 and to keep them out of American hands, a visiting officer took possession for the Crown in 1848.

The HBC obtained a contract to supply coal to the Pacific Mail Steamship Co. The first shipment went out in May 1849. It was quite a leap for the ancient fur-trading company. In the middle of it came the California Gold Rush. The demand for steam coal shot up.

That year also, Queen Victoria signed a grant making the directors of the HBC the "true lords and proprietors" of Vancouver Island and creating the Colony of Vancouver Island. The fine print stipulated that the grant could be revoked if the HBC did not establish a settlement within five years. The clock was ticking.

The HBC pinned its hopes on the Suquash mine. The company could have continued to buy coal but no — they chose to try to attract British miners to a watery wilderness at the ends of the earth, sneak them into the heartland of a warlike indigenous society under the noses of the owners and get them mining.

Impossible?

Company men arrived in Beaver Harbour in May 1849 to build sturdy Fort Rupert. The HBC continued to pay First Nations for coal, and within a few months James Douglas reported "most friendly relations with the natives who *without being acquainted with our future plans* are exceedingly useful in getting out coal." (Emphasis added.)

At Suquash, the miners dug 60 feet without finding a seam. When they did start taking out coal, armed First Nations people confronted them and demanded royalties.

The fort was in the middle of the ancient village site of *T'sakis*. Deserted at first, T'sakis soon had several thousand residents. The Kwakiutl were by nature assertive and observed customs that gave the settlers pause — like displaying the heads of their enemies.

Next spring the *Norman Morison* arrived with 80 immigrants. Miners and labourers raised a litany of grievances and were, James Douglas complained, "a troublesome useless sett." Soon most were on strike.

HBC officials treated it as a mutiny and clapped a few miners in irons. Some settlers had already thrown in the towel. Whole families were slipping away, California-bound.

The cargo ship *England* called in. Three men were aboard who had deserted the *Norman Morison*. When a magistrate came looking for them, they repaired to a nearby island. Soon it was reported they had been murdered. Two bodies were recovered. Kwakiutl informants pointed to Nahwitti people.

Into the fray waded the governor of Vancouver Island, Richard Blanshard, to bring the murderers to justice or, failing that, take revenge. "British blood never dries."

The other view was that British zeal to prosecute the killers might itself provoke an attack. After all, the men were AWOL employees of the Company. An HBC official may have put a price on their heads.

The merits of the case aside, Blanshard urged a demonstration of Resolve — or the fort, hugely outnumbered and weakened by internal strife, might be attacked.

HMS *Daedalus*, 20 guns, arrived with Blanshard aboard. A force was dispatched to a Nahwitti village. The village was deserted. Soon it was a smoking ruins.

In July 1851, Blanshard sailed north again in search of the murderers. The marines went to a Nahwitti village. During a brief battle — with a few casualties on both sides and one Nahwitti death — the residents vanished. Their houses and canoes were burned. The Nahwitti leaders negotiated a settlement. Some mutilated bodies were produced, and the case was closed.

Meanwhile, the Suquash coalbeds proved a bust. It took the HBC a year of searching to find the coal seams in Nanaimo Harbour and evacuate the brave coal miners and their families from Fort Rupert. The whole fiasco consumed nearly four years.

Apart from that, there was some good chemistry, and Fort Rupert remained open as an HBC fur-trading post, while the First Nations village became a great cultural centre.

Details: *the Suquash mine is owned by a Toronto mining company and is not open.*

T'sakis (Fort Rupert) is a major centre of Kwakwaka'wakw culture. The village took form around the Hudson's Bay Company's Fort Rupert. The First Nations community flourished and attracted intense study by anthropologists. For decades its arts and customs were minutely documented. The village became uniquely well-known. Today it remains the principal village of the Kwakiutl Indian Band — a crucible of art where visitors are welcome.

The story begins with George Hunt (1854-1933), who was born at Fort Rupert. Hunt's mother was a Tlingit chief's daughter from Alaska. His English father was an HBC trader. Hunt married into the village, having 11 children. He is the progenitor of the Hunt family artistic dynasty.

George Hunt was steeped in his adoptive culture and began collecting myths and regalia of the area. By the 1880s he was working as boatman, guide and interpreter with the Jessup North Pacific Expedition. Hunt spoke both English and Kwak'wala natively and sometimes worked as a court translator in Victoria.

In 1886 Franz Boaz, a young geographer working for a German museum, made the first of many trips to Vancouver Island to study First Nations people. Travelling up-island by steamer, he arrived in Nahwitti hoping to observe potlatch ceremonies. "At first they thought I was a priest, and now, because I had brought nothing, they thought I might be a government agent come to put a stop to the festival." The potlatch, an institution of gifting of central importance in Kwakwaka'wakw society, had recently been banned by the Canadian government. Boas told them he had come only to "see what the people in this land do."

In Victoria in 1888, Boas met George Hunt. Soon Boas's field work attracted funding from American museums to develop interpretations of Kwakiutl culture. The first collaboration of Boas and Hunt was of heroic proportions and caused a sensation.

In 1893, at Boas's invitation, George Hunt and 17 Fort Rupert Kwakiutl First Nation people traveled to Chicago. They shipped the timbers of a big house and an array of monumental carvings. Visitors to the six-month World's Columbian Exposition were treated to a recreated Kwakiutl village. (Some of the pieces are still standing in Chicago's Field Museum.)

The following year Boas visited Fort Rupert and witnessed the first weeks of the Winter Ceremonial, with George Hunt serving as guide and interpreter. Together they described the rituals and accoutrements of the round of singing, dancing, dramatization and story-telling, feasting, speech-making and potlatching at Fort Rupert. Nothing like it had ever been done.

Boas soon published the trailblazing *Social Organization and Secret Societies of the Kwakiutl Indians* (1897), which he prefaced thus: "The great body of facts presented here were observed and recorded by Mr. George

Hunt, who takes deep interest in everything pertaining the ethnology of the Kwakiutl Indians."

Researcher Judith Berman summarizes the collaboration: "Boas published some 15 books based on their collaborative Kwakwaka'wakw research." Of those, 11 "consist largely or exclusively of Hunt's Kwak'wala-language texts. While this work was not without flaws, probably no single ethnographic enterprise has documented a Native North American group as completely and from as many different angles."

Details: *T'sakis (Fort Rupert) is 39 km west of Port McNeill, 11 km east of Port Hardy: http://www.kwakiutl.bc.ca/index.htm*
This German website conveys something of the richness of Kwakwakawakw culture: http://www.firstnations.de/fisheries/kwakwakawakw.htm. Separate page about the Kwakiutl First Nation.

100 Cape Scott-North Coast Trail

Cape Scott Provincial Park protects 22,294 hectares of Vancouver Island's wild and isolated north end, including 115 kilometres of varied coast between San Josef Bay and Shushartie Bay. The extravagantly beautiful Cape Scott area has attracted wilderness trekkers since the park was established in 1973.

The north island is just beginning to tap its potential as an outdoor recreation destination. It's ideal for those who enjoy boating, kayaking, recreational fishing, hiking and wildlife viewing in remote landscapes. Scuba divers have already discovered the rich waters within God's Pocket Marine Provincial Park.

The supply centre is Port Hardy, a town of 4,000 at the terminus of Highway 19, 500 km north of Victoria. The trailhead for Cape Scott Park is on the San Josef River, 64 km west of Port Hardy on public and logging roads.

A 2.5-km trail to San Josef Bay has extensions (13 km) via Mt Patrick (422 m elevation) to Sea Otter Cove and Lowrie Bay. These relatively short, difficult trails lead to excellent camping areas. The main trail to Cape Scott is 23.6 hectares, and there's a 2-km side trail to Nissen Bight.

Some 90 Danish settlers moved into the Cape Scott area during the 1890s, but the farms produced little and remained isolated from markets. Many settlers left, and new populations moved in. A long-promised road never materialized, and the area was ultimately abandoned.

The challenging new North Coast Trail extends for 43 km between Nissen Bight and Shushartie Bay. Total length of the Cape Scott-North Coast Trail, trailhead to trailhead: about 58 km. There's no overland access to the eastern trailhead. You have to approach by water — a 35-km trip between Port Hardy and Shushartie Bay.

The new trail has been compared to the West Coast Trail in the 1970s. It is broken up-and-down terrain, with many steeply-pitched gravel beaches to walk. Allow for 10 km of travel a day. You have to be prepared for self-sufficient remote travel. Encounters with black bears are common.

The Cape Scott-North Coast Trail began with a vision of economic regeneration and the formation of the North Vancouver Island Trails Society. Some Port Hardy residents fundraised $1.2 million, about half of it community support money from the Feds to offset regional economic impacts. It took three years of heroic work by local volunteers to cut the trail. It's big news for wilderness trekkers.

Details: *Cape Scott Provincial Park, detailed maps, directions: http://www.env. gov.bc.ca/bcparks/explore/parkpgs/cape_scott/.*
Cape Scott Water Taxi and Marine Services, Port Hardy, operates land and water shuttles to trailheads: http://www.northcoasttrailshuttle.com/.
Exploring The North Coast Trail, an illustrated web-only guide: http://www.wild-coastmagazine.com/NorthCoastTrail.htm.
Cape Scott-North Coast Trail: http://www.clubtread.com/Routes/Route. aspx?Route=1188.

101   Triangle Island

Beyond Cape Scott, the northern tip of Vancouver Island, are Lanz and Cox islands. Then, in a line, the smaller Scott Islands: Beresford, Sartine and Triangle. The last island, Triangle, 46 kilometres N 81°W of Cape Scott, is a tiny dot on the face of the deep. The Scott islands are ecological reserves, closed to the public.

Triangle Island, to quote BC Parks' description, "supports over 400,000 breeding pairs of colonial seabirds — more than any other island on the British Columbia coast." Triangle, Beresford and Sartine islands comprise "the single most important seabird area in Pacific Canada."

Triangle hosts 40 percent of the world's population of Cassin's Auklet, an unimaginable 360,000 breeding pairs. Also "the largest and one of the few" Tufted Puffin colonies in BC, the largest Common Murre colony in BC, and the only known nesting site of Thick-billed Murres in Pacific Canada. A total of 81 bird species have been counted in the area.

According to Walbran's *Coast Names*, Triangle got its name from its three-cornered shape. The corners are strewn with rocks and reefs. The entire island has a vertiginous pitch — steep, steeper, vertical. Cliffs can be hidden by dense vegetation. Treeless, the island's dominant plant species is salmonberry, and the windswept plant community includes Pacific crabapple, tufted hairgrass and red elderberry.

Fortunately, we have a guide to this remarkably remote and inhospitable place. Biologist Alison Watt spent four months on Triangle Island at

indigo

chapters | indigo | indigo.ca

THANK YOU FOR YOUR ORDER.
WE HOPE YOU LOVE IT!

CUSTOMER SERVICE

SERVICE@CHAPTERS.INDIGO.CA
1 800 832 7569
MONDAY TO SUNDAY
9AM-12AM EASTERN
EASY RETURNS WITHIN 30 DAYS:
WWW.CHAPTERS.INDIGO.CA/FREE-RETURNS

JOIN THE CONVERSATION ON:

f @ ⓥ ⓟ f ⑧⁺ / @CHAPTERSINDIGO

#ASKINDIGO #INDIGOFAVES

---

indigo

chapters | indigo | indigo.ca

NOUS VOUS REMERCIONS POUR VOTRE COMMANDE.
NOUS ESPÉRONS QUE VOUS ALLEZ L'ADORER!

SERVICE À LA CLIENTÈLE

SERVICE@CHAPTERS.INDIGO.CA
1 800 832-7569
DU LUNDI AU DIMANCHE
DE 9 H À MINUIT, HE
RETOURS FACILES DANS LES 30 JOURS
WWW.CHAPTERS.INDIGO.CA/FREE-RETURNS

JOIGNEZ-VOUS À LA CONVERSATION SUR

f @ ⓥ ⓟ f ⑧⁺ / @INDIGOFRANCAIS

ORDER / COMMANDE: 60013906

DATE: November 1 2016

PAGE: 1 / 1

Kathie GellatlyCHAPTERS store # 0934

701 1ST AVE. S.

LETHBRIDGE, Alberta, T1J 4V7

Canada

ITEMS INCLUDED IN THE SHIPMENT

QTY	ITEM NAME	ITEM UPC
1	VANCOUVER ISLAND BK OF MUSTS	9780981094168

THANK YOU FOR CHOOSING INDIGO

PACK M: PKHU   SLOT/BIN :